how to start a home-based

Professional Organizing Business

HOME-BASED BUSINESS SERIES

how to start a home-based

Professional Organizing Business

Second Edition

Dawn Noble

gpp®

Guilford, Connecticut

This book is dedicated to all the future organizers out there that are excited to assist individuals and families in creating environments that are happier and healthier to live in.

Text design by Sheryl P. Kober

Library of Congress Cataloging-in-Publication Data is available on file.

ISBN 978-0-7627-6368-9

Printed in the United States of America
10 9 8 7 6 5 4 3 2 1

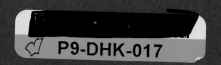

Contents

Acknowledgments

To my husband Chris: Always the biggest thank you goes to you. Your patience, grace, and simple way of taming my crazy astounds me. During a recent episode of crazy: final edits to the book, wallpaper half down, relatives coming to town, and our two little ones getting ready to start school, you simple kissed my forehead and said, "I knew what I was getting into when I said 'I Do.'" And for that safe place to fall, I thank you with all my heart.

Nicole, my oldest and organizer in training: I love the way you can turn on a smile in the middle of an upset and allow yourself to giggle when you want to cry. You're the reason I wanted a flexible work schedule in the first place and why I am so grateful I created one. Keep creating your lists and checking them twice. Follow your dreams and be happy. Mommy loves you.

Karli, my little observer and my second reason for wanting a flexible work schedule: Being around you makes me smile. A girl of few words you speak volumes with your spirit and happiness. Thank you for your hugs and gentleness. Follow your heart and be happy. Mommy loves you.

To my friend Kathy Smyly Miller: Thank you for walking with me on this journey. Your friendship means the world to me and makes me a better person each and every day. For my Mom: Not sure how to thank you for the way in which you just assume we'll all (me, Debbie, Carol Ann, and Frank) do great things. It makes it easier to get out there and do the things I want when you're behind me knowing I can. Thanks. For my Dad: You continue to amaze me with all you do. I can certainly see where I get my propensity for changing, learning, and creativity from. Thanks for being you. For friends A through, well, Z I suppose: thanks for being a part of my life and giving it such richness every day. It's always more fun when you have someone to say "how cool is that?" to at the end of a day. Thank you.

To the Globe Pequot Press family: Thank you for this series of home-based business books. I am fortunate to have the opportunity to be listed as the author of this particular title and appreciate your commitment to me and this work.

To the new professional organizers out there: congratulations, good luck, and thank you for your kind words of gratitude for the information I've provided in this book. I'm happy to know there are more organizers out there working their own bit of magic with people around the world.

Lastly, I'd like to thank all the clients who allow me into their worlds to share, learn, grow, and experience this passion of mine. I truly enjoy every minute with you and am grateful you open your world and trust me to support you on this journey.

Introduction

As my husband walked out the door for his yearly golf adventure in the Carolinas, I told him that by the time he returned I would have made a decision about my career. This came after a year of self-imposed unemployment, due to my decision to leave a nursing job that was financially rewarding but emotionally exhausting—so demanding that it took a toll on my health. My husband gone, the house quiet, I was now alone with my thoughts.

How was I going to create a work life that was everything I wanted it to be? And what was it that I wanted, anyway? I went for a drive, the questions racing through my head. *What would I love to do tomorrow? Could lose track of time doing? And wouldn't care if someone paid me or not?* The answer: Clean out a closet.

I thought, *Now, who in their right mind would answer the question that way? There's got to be something to this.* I rushed home to search my bookshelf and found several books I had purchased on the subject of organizing. I turned one book over to read about the author and noticed the title of professional organizer. *What is that?* I wondered. As I investigated, on the Internet and at the bookstore, I discovered there was an association for these professional organizers. I began reading anything I could put my hands on about what they did. They clean out closets...and basements, and kitchens, and playrooms, and offices...oh my! So there *are* people out there who are as passionate about cleaning and organizing as I am. Who knew? At that moment I knew the direction my future work life would take.

The minute my husband arrived home, I rushed to him and said, "I'll be cleaning out closets for a living!"

He smiled and said, "I don't get it, but if it makes you happy, go for it."

So there I was, with this idea that felt so right and exciting, but no clue how to get started.

My first action was to call the company owned by the author of one of the books I had been reading, to see if I could work with them to get some experience in the field of organizing. I interviewed, got about six hours of training, and off I went to work with clients. I left the house each morning excited about the chaos I was about to discover and help the client sift through. The experience was everything I thought it would be . . . messy closets, disorganized basements, dumping-ground garages, and overgadgeted kitchens. The paperwork piles, stacks of unopened mail, and boxes and bags stuffed with all types of paper would be frightful for most, but for me they were a puzzle waiting to be pieced together—and I enjoyed each part of the process. I especially liked working one-on-one with my clients. Whether it was in a corporate setting or private home, the dynamics were the same, and it was very fulfilling.

The one unfortunate aspect of my dream job was that the company was located in another state, and my commute was brutal. I had to find a way to continue this work that I loved, but closer to home. I looked into apprenticing with someone closer, but couldn't find anyone offering organizing services anywhere nearby.

After having dinner with a friend one evening, during which there was much soul-searching conversation and admittedly a few drinks, I realized that I had the commitment and drive to start my own business. Buoyed by the passion that I felt for organizing and the support of my husband, family, and friends, I began researching what it would take to get my business started. It was overwhelming. *Where do I start? How much money do I need? How will I find clients? Will I make any money doing this? Do I need more training than I've gotten during my short stint working part-time as an apprentice?* These questions and more kept me awake night after night.

Now, eleven years and thousands of clients later, I am here to provide you with a clear path to starting your very own home-based professional organizing business. This book will tell you everything you need to know, the good, the bad, and the ugly. I realize now that if there had been a resource available to me such as the one you're reading today, it would have relieved me of many sleepless nights and many mistakes along the way. I would have gotten to the business of organizing much sooner—and would have been earning an income much sooner as well. I am excited to be sharing this information with you. If you are committed to your dream and follow the steps outlined in this book, you will be successful and fulfilled in this business in a very short period of time.

First, we'll look at your decision to start your own business and make sure you have the passion and determination to thrive in this field. We'll talk about what training you need and how you can get yourself credibility in the marketplace. We'll discuss what it takes to run a business and test your commitment to this sometimes daunting task. We'll examine the money it takes to get started, and once you've determined that you're all set, you'll put together a simple, but essential, business plan that will capture your passion on paper and keep you going through the rough times.

Did I say rough times? Well, yes, there will be times and tasks that aren't much fun. For me it was the financial accounting and the myriad details of setting up a business; I just wanted to get to the closets. But I knew then and I know now that establishing the structure of my business was critical to my ultimate success. So we will work together to set up the "hardware" of your home-based business, everything from the phone lines to your filing system. I'll deal directly with how to set up the business entity itself, walking you through the decision of whether to be a sole proprietor, an LLC, or a DBA. You'll have the chance to come up with the name of your company and learn what the local and federal issues are. I'll also provide you with simple financial recording forms that make tax preparation a breeze. I'll help you get the look you want for your business, from logo to brochure design to web presence. I will give you formulas for setting your rates and establishing your policies for working with clients. In this book you will find sample forms and templates onto which you can just drop your logo and be ready to go.

Go where? you ask. To your first client, of course!

The thought of marketing your new business may be mind-boggling, and after you make your first call to price an ad in a local magazine or newspaper, you'll probably fall off your chair. But there are many solutions for you to consider. I'll help you put together a marketing plan that will take into account both your budget and your style. I'll tell you about marketing and networking opportunities that yield results right away.

A major concern for new professional organizers is the ability to get new clients during challenging economic times; this is a realistic concern, especially when your hourly rate gets up there. What I tell those getting started in the business, and what I remind myself of routinely, is that the service I provide is just as valuable in difficult times as it is in good times. The need for me to focus my marketing may be more critical during a downturn to isolate the clients I feel are my target market. I will share with you the adjustments I have made along the way and techniques that I use to target my market.

Once the clients start calling, you will be ready to make your first visit—and you will need support and confidence to do this. You'll find in these pages a step-by-step guide to walk you through the initial assessment with the client as well as a foolproof formula for working with any client and for any organizing situation, at any time. Supplied with this formula, you'll never be at a loss when you're out there with clients. I'll help you polish the skills you currently have and enhance your knowledge in the products area. You will be armed with a resource list of products as well as complementary services your client may need.

We'll also talk about the prospect of growing your business when the time comes. Once you realize the potential for growth and the ease with which you can manage your career from home, you'll know exactly what to do if you choose to expand.

The satisfaction you'll receive from helping your clients achieve simplicity and organization in their lives is very rewarding. Even more rewarding will be your pride at watching your very own business grow and thrive. It's all possible if you follow the steps I've outlined in this book.

Congratulations on your decision to embark on this wonderful journey. Let's get started!

01 So You Think You Want to Be a Professional Organizer?

You're visiting with a friend as she searches through her kitchen cabinets, mumbling, "I know it's here somewhere, I just saw it the other day." You see her stuffing the tumbled-out plastic containers back into the cabinet she just opened as she complains that her kitchen is just too small. You itch to help her sift through those containers, knowing how much time and energy you could save her by creating better order. You daydream about how much simpler her life would be if she would just put that over here and this over there. You can't help it—you offer a suggestion or two...and before you know it, you're both knee deep in the cabinets and the kitchen looks like a disaster. For you it's a visit to a playground; for her it's a nightmare come to life! Yet as the afternoon progresses, she begins to see results and is amazed at how much space has been created and how nice her cabinets look. She says, "I feel like I can breathe easier." You leave feeling exhilarated and energized and wanting more!

Does any of this sound familiar? Have you found yourself staying up late to watch those cable TV shows in which organizers and designers drastically transform someone's home or office space? Do you find yourself wandering through container stores and office supply stores or sifting through catalogs that carry organizational supplies, happily imagining storage solutions for yourself, your family, your friends, the local convenience store, your office, wherever? Do you walk into a room and find yourself reorganizing the furniture, cabinets, and containers in your head? If you love the sense of calm and efficiency that comes with a well-ordered space and would like to put your talents to good use, you might like to be a professional organizer—but you're going to have to answer some tough questions first. It's one thing to be passionate about organizing; it's another to do it for a living. First take this quiz, then we'll check back in.

Are You Ready to Become a Professional Organizer?

Answer yes or no to the following questions:

- Does the thought of cleaning out a closet put a smile on your face?
- Do you look forward to the end result of cleaning or organizing a space?
- Can you visualize an organized space even in the midst of the clutter?
- Can you visually measure space and approximate how many containers will fit into a particular spot?
- Have you ever suggested to a friend, "I can come over this weekend and help you organize that closet"?
- Do you feel comfortable offering suggestions that will dramatically change how a space looks or functions?
- Are you creative and innovative enough to come up with several different solutions to one problem?
- Do you have a sense of humor?
- Do you have compassion for the disorganized person?
- Can you clearly explain your ideas?
- Can you see situations and instinctively know how to make them easier and simpler?
- Do you get excited when you see a messy or disorganized space, knowing the potential for change?
- Are you passionate about organizing?

So how did you do? If you answered yes to many of the questions, then you're well on your way to creating an exciting and rewarding career for yourself.

If you're anything like me, you may be wondering right now: *Will people really pay me to rid them of messy closets and basements and paper piles 3 feet high? How will I get started? Am I really capable of running my own business?*

Well, we're going to find out in the next couple of pages. This first chapter is designed to give you a glimpse of your very near future should you choose to start your own home-based professional organizing business. You can be ready to see your first client in two weeks, or you can take your time putting the pieces in place and ease into working with your first client. Either way you will build a strong foundation for your business and your professional future.

What Is a Professional Organizer?

If you asked this question a decade ago, you would have been met with blank stares and shrugs. These days, however, thanks to cable television and the many books and magazine articles out there about organizing and clearing clutter, professional organizers have hit the mainstream. We're now regularly being sought out by people desperate for help with their home environment as well as their office space.

So what is a professional organizer? It's someone who provides information, products, and support (hands-on or not) to individuals, families, and businesses large or small, assisting them in creating a simpler, more efficient work or living space. We help clients assess their current situation and together create a plan to build a healthier environment. It may be in the form of a closet organizer, a better filing system, or a kitchen cabinet pullout. It may be a way for clients to organize their daily tasks better or to complete their work assignments with more efficiency. Whatever form it takes, it is up to the professional organizer to use creativity and skill to design a better-organized, simpler environment for clients.

The environment an organizer creates should reflect who clients are and what's important to them; it should match their needs and make living and working easier on a daily basis. We organizers want our clients to get on with the business of living life instead of just surviving it. So where does the "professional" part come in? You probably think it denotes some formal training, licensing, or experience. What *professional* really means, though, is that you're getting paid for the work you do. Once you accept that first check for providing information, assistance, and products that help folks increase their efficiency, organize their space, manage their time, or

"But What Is It That You Do?"

From your first mention that you are going into business for yourself, you'll be selling your services. It helps to have a fifteen- to thirty-second response to the question, *What is it that you do?* Since most people have seen or heard of professional organizers at this point, thanks to the wonderful world of cable television, it's much easier to explain. "I'm a professional organizer. I help people create systems that keep things running smoothly at work and at home." That's been the simplest version I have come up with.

otherwise be more productive, congratulations—you are a professional organizer! There are other traits that characterize a professional, of course: honesty, integrity, credibility...all of these and more add to your overall package of professionalism.

What Certifications, Skills, or Training Do You Need?

All of the above notwithstanding, when a clients asks you "What makes you a professional organizer?" you'll want to answer with something more reassuring than "I get paid"! Let's look at how you might establish your bona fides in this field.

Certifications

What type of certification does a professional organizer need? None. There is no organization or governing body that states who can and cannot become a professional organizer. There *are* organizations that have been established to support the profession and to assist you in learning about the trade; however, their training programs and certification programs are strictly voluntary. The National Association of Professional Organizers (NAPO), Professional Organizers in Canada (POC), and National Study Group on Chronic Disorganization (NSGCD) are three such organizations. NAPO and NSGCD both have certification processes in place. The NAPO certification exam is based on eligibility requirements, including prior organizing experience and proof of independent education along with an exam. NSGCD's certification is an exam based on its own educational program specific to the chronically disorganized client. Both groups offer programs and courses that are helpful in learning about the professional organizing trade and will provide you with basic information needed to pass their particular exam. That said, it is up to you whether you would like to have certification status. To date I have not gone through either certification process. It's not that I don't qualify, don't believe I can pass, or don't believe in the concept of certification; it's more about my need in my day-to-day business for this acknowledgment or head nod from these associations and what it can do for me. You need to decide if this is something that you would like to have to "prove" your status as a professional. Some clients will be looking for individuals who have completed a study program, but it has been my experience that our type of business grows largely through word of mouth, and most clients will come to you based on the experience a friend or colleague has had with you, not solely on whether you have a certificate or not. Remember, certification does not guarantee quality. Quality is about your dedication and application of learned or experienced knowledge.

There is no official college degree or schooling for this profession, and professional organizers come from a variety of backgrounds. Still, family, friends, your accountant or attorney (should you choose to use one), and certainly potential clients will want to know about how you learned how to do this job. As one friend put it: "What makes you think you can do this for people and get paid for it?" Interesting question, and one that I knew would be important to have a credible answer for. I was convinced I could help people become better organized and create more efficient environments. I had read many books on the subject, and I even worked for a professional organizer for several months. So all I really needed to do was to put this information together, polish it up a bit, and get comfortable talking about it in such a way as to inspire others to have the same confidence in me that I had in myself.

Skills and Qualifications

So here's an exercise I've created to help you identify your skills and qualifications for becoming an organizer. Pull out an old résumé or take a minute to list any and all jobs you have had. List any organizing talents you needed to complete your duties in these positions, such as customer service, event coordination, design of new work procedures, management of employees—any job function that required you to design and create solutions. Think about any classes you may have taken, volunteer work, association memberships, and leadership roles; all of this experience counts! The following questions may help you remember any times in which you used your organizing skills:

Gaining Experience

"Getting organizing experience is easy—there are opportunities all around," says Ruthann Betz-Essinger, owner of Just Organized, LLC. "I do free work for local charities. They refer families to me that have been in for counseling or support, and I get to help people who really need it but otherwise would probably not be able to afford it. Some pay, some don't; it all depends on their situation. I also have a relationship with a doctor who treats ADD patients. He will often refer them to me if there's something he believes I can help with."

- What inspired you to begin the process of becoming a professional organizer?
- What type of organizing do you love to do?
  Have you taken any workshops or seminars on organizing or time management?
- What books have you read on organizing? List them.
- Where do you feel you are best organized: home, office, paperwork, time management, moving coordination, event coordination?
- List your organizing projects, whether free or paid, with friends or family.
- How did you organize these situations or events? What approach did you take? Be as specific as you can.

As you write down your answers, leave extra space so you can add information as you continue to recall other times when you organized someone or something. Of course, if someone asks you about your credentials, you're not going to begin reciting from this list; it will simply be a mental resource that you draw from to maintain your confidence as you start your new business. You can include this information in your online bio, as well as your company profile.

Typical Backgrounds for Organizers

- Administrative assistant
- Financial consultant
- Hotel and restaurant management
- Massage therapist
- Nurse
- Teacher

Now, having learned that there is no organization or governing body placing restrictions on who can become a professional organizer, and having identified and listed your skills and qualifications, how do you feel? If this exercise confirmed that you have a passion for organizing, as I suspect you do, and you are willing to continue learning the trade and polishing your skills (which I'll cover in detail in chapter 4), then you are ready to move on to the next question.

Professional Societies for Organizers

- National Association of Professional Organizers (NAPO): www.NAPO.net
- Professional Organizers Web Ring: www.organizerswebring.com
- Professional Organizers in Canada (POC): www.organizersincanada.com

What Type of Organizing Should You Do?

The answer to this question is simple: *Do what you love*. I'm assuming the main reason you struck out on this journey to become a professional organizer is because it's something you love to do. So why stop now? If there is an area of organizing or type of client that appeals strongly to you, then you'll do your best work there. If you like working with stay-at-home moms who need help with their kitchens, playrooms, and schedules, for instance, then have at it. If your interest is in working with self-employed businesspeople in desperate need of someone to design a workflow and paper-management system for the small office, then that's where you should be. This is especially true at the beginning of your journey. You want to be working with the clients you feel the most comfortable with so you can hone your skills and continue to learn as you go.

So answer this question as quickly as you can: What type of organizing would you love to do tomorrow, would you do for free, and would make you lose track of time?

Now look at the following lists on page 8 and check any and all types of organizing you would feel confident tackling and types of clients that you would be excited to work with. Remember, as you grow your business, you will also increase your experience level and be able to work with a wider variety of clients if you choose. For now, though, stick with what you know best: You'll grow your business that much quicker and with that much more confidence and success.

Types of Projects	Types of Clients
❏ Home organizing	❏ Individuals
❏ Attics	❏ Families
❏ Basements	❏ Children
❏ Kitchens	❏ Multiples (twins, triplets, what have
❏ Playrooms	you)
❏ Bedrooms	❏ Teenagers
❏ Garages	❏ Students
❏ Closets	❏ Seniors
❏ Collections, memorabilia, photos	❏ Executives
❏ Family management	❏ Self-employed
❏ Filing systems—home	❏ Home-based business owners
❏ Filing systems—business	❏ Corporations
❏ Garage sales	❏ Disabled persons
❏ Time and task management	❏ Other
❏ Office—home	
❏ Office—commercial	
❏ Computer management	
❏ Downsizing	
❏ Moving	
❏ Space planning	
❏ Storage/warehouse	
❏ Wardrobe consulting	
❏ Interior design	

The more flexible you are when you first start to see clients, the more you will learn and the better you'll be able to identify what specific areas of organizing you like and don't like. Ultimately, it will be important to have an idea of the types of organizing you enjoy most so that you can direct your marketing efforts toward those areas. Don't get too worried about this yet, however. Certainly, know your limits. You never want to take on a client you do not have the expertise for, but stretching yourself a bit each time you take on a new project is good for you.

In choosing the types of clients you are willing to work with, keep in mind that each will have a unique personality. For instance, you may be comfortable working with teenagers, but working with a straight-A student who needs to prepare for college is very different from working with a teen in danger of being left behind due to poor grades and disruptive behavior. We'll talk more about personality types later in the book. In particular, chapter 4 will give you a formula for handling every type of client, one that will help you in unfamiliar territory.

Remember that there is nothing wrong with working with clients for a portion of a job, then referring them to another professional. I once worked with a career coach based out of her home. We organized her office, creating a new filing system, a place to meet clients, and an office supply area, along with a few other small projects. But when it came time to deal with her computer system, I knew instantly I was out of my comfort zone. I referred her to a reliable computer-training professional. This client was thrilled with the work we had done together, and happy that I was able to refer her to someone with the computer expertise she needed. Sure, I could learn about computer software and applications myself, but why? Remember what I said earlier: Do what you love. Well, that's exactly what I do, and it serves me and my clients well.

How Do You Set Up a Business?

There are many things to think about and decisions to be made in the beginning, but in general this is an easy business to set up and maintain. The toughest part for most business owners is staying organized, but since that is your area of expertise, once you're set up it should be a breeze!

In the coming chapters I will explain each step you must take when setting up your business, as well as the pros and cons for all the options you'll be considering. I'll also share with you what has worked for me and other professional organizers. Additionally, I have provided websites and other resources to check out if you need to delve into any particular area.

For now, as you're setting up your new venture, the most important question to ask is not how to do it; it's "How do I know I can run a business?" Get ready to explore the depths of your commitment!

How Do You Know You Can Run a Business?

You may be passionate about organizing and have the skills to do so, but if you're not ready to seriously put your nose to the grindstone, your business will struggle. *Wait a minute,* you're thinking. *Didn't she just say that this is an easy business to start?* Well, yes, in that it doesn't take much overhead or educational preparation. But don't kid yourself: Starting any business, even one as fun and rewarding as organizing, takes discipline, patience, tenacity, and lots of energy.

That said, let's start out with a simple test of your readiness to become a business owner.

What Does It Take to Be a Business Owner?

On a scale of 1 through 10 (10 being the highest), evaluate yourself on these characteristics:

_____ Self-starter

_____ Focused

_____ Passionate about this idea

_____ Innovative

_____ Adaptable

_____ Confident

_____ People oriented

_____ Problem solver

_____ Goal-oriented

_____ Risk taker

_____ Persuasive

_____ Resourceful

_____ Honest

_____ Creative

- If your score is between 110 and 140, you're ready to become an entrepreneur.
- If your score is between 90 and 110, you're almost ready to become an entrepreneur.
- If your score is between 70 and 90, you should probably find an organizer to work for before striking out on your own.
- If your score is less than 70, you might want to think whether this is the right career path for you.

If you've scored well enough to identify yourself as an entrepreneur, then you're ready to hear the good, the bad, and the ugly about being in business for yourself. So here goes: It's time consuming, it's stressful, it's challenging, and it will work you even when you're sleeping. It invades your home life and makes you do things you don't want to do. Your income is erratic, your vacations unpaid, your health benefits nonexistent, and you'll find it hard to maintain balance between work and home. Are you still there? I haven't lost you yet? If you can deal with these definite downsides, you probably have the stomach for this venture.

Now I'll let you in on the joys of being a home-based business owner: It's flexible, it's rewarding, it's exciting, and it can be put on hold when you need time to yourself. You take tremendous pride in what you do, you have total creative control, you create your own hours, you're living your dream. You can do laundry in between business calls. It's all that and more!

You will have to wear many hats as a business owner, some of which may not fit very well. It is important to know where your strengths and weaknesses are, and when to ask for help. When it comes to marketing, for instance, you need to be able to sell yourself as a professional and to obtain clients regularly. If that's difficult for

Colleagues' Corner

Claire O'Connor, founder, Enchanted Home, LLC
First step: "Organizing for friends and family, getting testimonials and pictures of the before-and-after from those projects."
Biggest fear: Having started in the business when it was still a relatively unknown service, Claire wondered, "Will people really pay me for something that seems so natural to me?" Luckily those fears were quickly allayed.
Greatest challenge: "Feeling connected to others in the same boat." As an entrepreneur you're often on your own to make decisions, be creative, and blaze a trail, but Claire reports, "It's extremely important to nourish and sustain connections with other entrepreneurs, both within and outside the industry."
Hottest tip: "Don't reinvent the wheel when you're getting started. Reach out and seek the counsel of those who've gone before you, and don't be afraid to pay for their expertise. It's been more than worth it to my business when I've done so."

you, you'll need to identify this weakness before it starts to negatively affect your income. Later in the book I'll cover marketing extensively—it's a large component in the success of your business. If you can identify early on that you struggle with sales, you'll be better equipped to compensate by hiring someone to help you, or you can engage in marketing and/or advertising methods that allow you to remain behind the scenes. Then again, you may find that you're quite comfortable speaking with and in front of people when you are talking about something you love!

Recommended Resource

Need help visualizing your start-up costs in relation to your personal expenses? A tool I highly recommend is *Too Busy to Budget* by Kathy Miller, A Good Steward, LLC. The financial planning system presented in this book simplifies bill paying and creates a great visual image telling you exactly where you stand with your finances. To learn more, visit www.agoodsteward.net.

What Will This Cost You?

The two lists on pages 14 and 15 will give you a realistic idea of how much money you'll need to get started and to maintain your business every month. Review each item and determine whether you already have it in place or would need to make a purchase. I have estimated a total of approximately $8,000 to launch your business, but my guess is that you have some of these items already. For example, look at the budgeted estimates. I have allotted for a professional web design, whereas you may be the creative type and have the technical skills to establish your own basic web presence. So you could funnel that estimated cost into another category for now; then, when your budget allows, you could hire someone to professionally design your site. I think you will be pleasantly surprised by these lists. Starting up a professional organizing business isn't very expensive and can be done in stages.

Another financial detail you need to consider right off the bat is income. If you're coming off a full-time paid position with benefits, you could well pay a heavy cost in terms of income in the beginning. Remember, you're not working twenty or forty hours a week with clients to start with. If you are the primary income earner for your household, you will have to determine how to effect this start-up gradually. Plenty of clients will be available in the evenings or weekends, for example, so it might make sense to keep your day job while working with organizing clients nights and weekends until you have a solid client base and can determine which advertising is working to bring you more. Or you could continue working part-time as you get your new business under way. But if you can survive with limited income, or have limited time to devote to work hours—perhaps you have children to care for—you can start your organizing business with just one client and progress from there.

When I started, I had been out of work for a year, so we were used to surviving on one income. Business start-up, however, was an additional expense. As small as this was, we felt the pinch when it came time to pay the bills every month. In retrospect, I wish I had thought to create a calendar that forecast when I'd need money and when I could expect to start bringing it in. This kind of schedule would have allowed me to pace myself and not create more pressure on my personal life.

If you need to start your business slowly, that's okay. If getting your phone line installed and business cards printed is all you can do right now, fine. Just get out there and get some clients; when the money starts coming in, then you can move on with the other items you need.

Other Costs

In addition to the toll your new venture will take on your finances, there are other costs for you to consider when starting up a business.

Mental

Starting a business will be challenging and sometimes overwhelming. There are many decisions to make, and you will be learning about the business world at a breakneck pace. You need a clear mind and accountability to a list to succeed in making business decisions. Using a tool like this book for guidance is one way to support yourself through the process. More resources may include other professional organizers, contacts from any associations or organizations you've joined, or fellow entrepreneurs who've been in business for a while and are doing it successfully. Whoever your resources are, make contact, ask for help, and follow up with a thank-you once you've reached a decision in a difficult area.

Start Up Costs

Expense	Estimated Amount	What You Already Have in Place	What You Need
Vehicle/transportation	variable	_____	_____
Website design	$500	_____	_____
Post office box	$25	_____	_____
Telephone line	$150	_____	_____
Voice mail/answering service	$75	_____	_____
Cell phone	$100	_____	_____
Computer	$600	_____	_____
Printer	$150	_____	_____
Desk and chair	$250	_____	_____
Filing cabinets	$100	_____	_____
Contact database program	$150	_____	_____
Word-processing software	$150	_____	_____
Camera (digital preferred)	$200	_____	_____
Workbag and contents	$200	_____	_____
Office supplies	$150	_____	_____
Stationery/Business cards	$250	_____	_____
Banking fees	$35	_____	_____
Business entity filing	variable	_____	_____
Insurance	$250	_____	_____
Advertising	$1,500	_____	_____
Association fees (optional)	$320	_____	_____
Legal fees (optional)	$1,000	_____	_____
Accounting fees (optional)	$600	_____	_____
Resources and coaching (optional)	$600	_____	_____
Training and education (optional)	variable	_____	_____
Accounting software (optional)	$180	_____	_____
Total	$7,635 **Your total**	_____	_____

Operating Costs

Item	Monthly Average
Accounting/bookkeeping	$25
Advertising	$200+
Banking fees	$20
Cell phone	$55+
Insurance premiums	$50
Phone line	$35
Post office box	$10
Supplies—office	$25
Supplies—work bag	$35
Web hosting	$40
Total	$495 per month

Emotional

Starting your own business is exciting and can be very rewarding. Just a few pages back, you took a test to determine if you were ready to become a business owner. If you did not score well but are sure you can muddle through—think again. This venture will take an emotional toll on you and your family if you are not prepared. On the flip side, if you are ready to go on this journey, then you are in for the ride of a lifetime. Combining your passion for organizing with your ambition to start a business can create one of the most rewarding experiences of your lifetime. I sometimes think of the launch of my business as akin to the birth of a baby. It was a profound and rewarding experience that I will cherish and be proud of forever.

Spiritual

How can starting your own business be spiritual? You'll find out shortly when you're down on your knees praying for a new client to call! There's part humor and part reality in that statement. I remember checking my phone messages numerous times the day after I'd completed a mailing, just praying someone would call. You will be challenged on the deepest levels, whether by a difficult client, trying to build your client base, or searching for an address in the midst of a rainstorm. Wherever you gather your inner strength, make sure you have it in place as you embark on this journey.

Physical

Believe it or not, this is a very physical job. Up to now you've probably done organizing work with friends and family at your own pace. When you're working with clients, however, you're on the clock. No, you don't have to sprint around their offices or homes, but you will be moving constantly from the time you arrive to the time you leave. Add in the mental exercise of keeping one step ahead of clients in the organizing process, and you've got a job that will take a toll on your body. I often found that I was so excited to be working with clients, I didn't even feel the fatigue until I got back home and tried to climb out of my car. So a word to the wise: Get out there and start pumping iron, take a yoga class, do something physical now to prepare yourself.

How Much Money Can You Make?

There's no single, simple answer to this question. Instead, your income potential depends on a variety of factors. Will you be working full-time or part-time? With private clients or corporate? What is your experience level, and what is your comfort

The Rate Debate

I've had many e-mails asking for assistance regarding setting rates: "In an economy like this," "in the area that I live," "because of the competition...." I always refer new organizers back to the formula. Yes, you can start out at a lower rate; however, raising your rates may prove to be difficult—as word-of-mouth is one of your greatest marketing opportunities, people share not only what it is you do, they share what it is you charge. You need to be sure your starting rates allow your business to be sustainable. If you can't cover your expenses (business and personal as needed), you may find yourself out of business before you even get started!

zone with your prices? Organizers charge $50 to $150 per hour for residential or personal organizing; $75 to $200 or more per hour for business organizing. Corporations will pay $1,000 to $3,000 per day, or even more, depending on the project, service, or organizer.

To figure out where you might fall on the fee schedule, first determine how many hours you'd like to work a week and the total income you'd like to have. Here's the formula:

Desired total income = $50,000
40 hours per week = 20 client/billable hours per week
20 billable hours x 45 weeks (subtracting vacation days, sick days,
       holidays) = 900 hours per year
$50,000 ÷ 900 hours = $55 per hour

This rate falls within the average and could be a good starting point. As your experience level grows, so will your fee structure. Add speaking fees, workshops, and corporate clients to this mix and your income can grow exponentially.

Chapter 5 will go into much more detail about setting your rates.

How Do You Find Clients?

Clients are all around you, every day. Most of us have "Get organized" at the top of our list of resolutions each new year. People are forever making comments like "If I just had more time . . ." or "If I were only more organized . . ." Almost everyone is looking for ways to increase productivity in all areas of their lives. They want to know how to do things easier and faster. As professional organizers, it's our job to assist individuals and families in evaluating their current situations and creating a plan to live more simply and more efficiently. There isn't a person out there who couldn't use our assistance!

That said, it's really up to clients to find you. What I mean is that a client who seeks out your services is one who's excited and ready to begin the journey to a simpler, more organized life. I have been asked and have refused to offer gift certificates for my services. Why? Because giving the gift of professional organizing services is like telling people they need to go on a diet! No one wants to hear that from anyone, no matter how loving a gesture the gift giver may think it is. Let clients find you when they're ready for you.

They'll hear about you through your advertising, through your marketing, and through word of mouth. (I'll cover all these topics in detail in chapter 6.) As your business grows, so does your client base. The old adage, "... and *they* tell two friends, and *they* tell two friends, and so on, and so on...," is very true in this field. Organizing is a personal business. You are dealing with personal issues and possessions. People who've had good experiences with you will refer you to others and talk about you in their everyday lives. So my suggestion to you is to make the following one of your business affirmations: *When I've laid down the proper groundwork, clients will find me when they're ready.*

Why We Do It

When asked, "Why do you do it?" Galye Gruenberg from Get Organized Now answered: "Being a professional organizer is the ultimate career in which one can give and receive. I do what I love every day. I touch people's lives and connect with them on a deep level. I share my talents and make a difference in the world. I am the captain of my own ship. I spend time with my children. I learn something new every day and stay sharp. I create a rich, full, and rewarding life for myself, my family, and my clients. I am grateful."

Kathy Smyly Miller, entrepreneur states: "We all have gifts. As entrepreneurs we get to share our gifts every day and make a living while making a difference. We also have challenges, and by facing them and growing through them, we have more to offer our clients. Thank you for doing what you do. Your contribution and commitment to your clients creates a stronger community. Kathy Smyly Miller, entrepreneur, www.kathysmylymiller.com

Where Do You Go from Here?

If you've made it to this point in the chapter and haven't been scared off yet, you must have the passion and the readiness to embark on this wonderful journey. It's just a matter of time and dedication before you'll have your business off the ground. What I'd like to ask you to do now is to create your business plan. Don't panic—it's not as painful as you'd think. Creating a business plan is simply a matter of asking yourself some questions and putting your answers in writing.

I have read many books on getting started in business, and there's one thing they have in common: They all mention the importance of the business plan. Some call it an *executive summary*, a *market analysis*, a *sales forecast*...big yawn, long stretch. One of the books even said, "A normal business plan should be between 30 and 50 pages." Yikes! Call me abnormal, but I'd like to see you create a business plan that captures your excitement, enthusiasm, and passion for the business you're about to start, and I'd like you to do it in one page. Yes, I understand that once you reach the point of seeking out financing to grow your business, you'll need to bulk up this plan (just as all the other books talk about). You're not doing that right now, though. Right now you're getting started, and one page is all you need.

Grab some paper and answer the following questions with the first thoughts that come to your mind:

- **What are you creating?** Describe your business in your words. When someone asks what it is you do, what do you hear yourself saying?
- **Why are you creating this?** Be honest and truthful. Do you love baskets and bins and cleaning up messes? Do you appreciate the fact that you can make money at it? Whatever it is, write down why you are creating this business.
- **What are your objectives or goals?** Be as specific as you can. For example, your goal might be: *To have ten to fifteen client hours per week by the end of June, Fridays off, a flexible schedule.* This may be easier at the end of the book when you're armed with more information, but get what you can down on paper now. It'll be fun to see the difference in only a short time.
- **How will you build your business?** What types of clients are you after? What are your ideas for generating clients? (These are the basics. As for advertising, speaking, networking—we'll get you to the specifics of those later.)
- **What is your plan?** What are the steps you will need to take to get to your goals?

You don't need to be perfect in what you say here—just write it down and move on. This portion may include a timeline of how you see it unfolding. Simply getting your thoughts into writing makes a great start. And you can (and hopefully will) come back to this plan later and add to it. This should be a working document that is ever changing in the first months to a year of starting your business. I suggest pinning it up on the wall and reviewing it often to see where you are. Write on this copy any ideas and changes that have occurred during the process, and create an updated version every month or so.

02 | Setting Up Your Office

Getting set up for business at home is a simple process that can be completed pretty quickly if you stay focused. This chapter will walk you through each step and provide you with the information you need to make each decision that comes up along the way.

Step by step we'll establish your office space, gather your supplies, design your filing system, and consider client-management products. Then I'll help you think about the look of your company logo, business cards, and website. You'll want to start a to-do list: By the time we're through, you're going to have a lot of things you'll want to take care of as soon as possible.

A few things to remember: First, go with your gut—if you're faced with several options, choose the one that suits you best. Second, don't forget that you can always make changes later on. Finally, remember that you're doing this because you enjoy organizing—and you'll get to do that once the business stuff is out of the way!

Office Space in Your Home

When you're thinking about your office space, it makes sense to determine what your needs are *right now* and not get caught up in what you might need three years from now. You'll see that by starting out with what you need immediately, your business and office space will grow with you and suit your needs every step of the way.

So with that in mind, what are the basics? It almost goes without saying that you'll need a phone, along with a computer to create and save client records, forms, and a database. Of course, you can do this by hand, but I'd only recommend that for the true technophobe. You'll also need a chair, a proper desk, paper, and some file folders. That's about it. Very basic and simple.

Okay, who am I kidding, I'm talking to a professional organizer, right? You want a list and you want to be able to check it twice. Here is a detailed list of what you'll need:

- Hanging folders: V-style folders 1-inch box-bottom folders and 2-inch box-bottom folders. (I prefer Smead brand.)
- File folders: Smead two-ply colored 1/3-cut letter folders (one color for each category—more on this later in the chapter)
- File folders: Any brand of manila 1/3-cut letter folders, all the same tab
- Printer paper (8.5 by 11 inches)
- Pencils
- Pencil sharpener
- Pens
- Scissors
- Stapler and staples
- Tape
- Garbage can
- Legal pads
- Spiral notebook (8.5 by 11 inches) (I dedicate this notebook to incoming calls. As I answer the phone I reach for it and write everything down as I'm talking. Later I capture this information in its appropriate spot, put a line through it in the notebook, and keep it for reference.)
- Daytimer or PDA (whatever you use for your calendar)
- Calculator
- Label maker
- Label maker tape
- Phone: One or two lines
- Headset for hands-free phone calls
- Computer
- Computer software (I'll discuss this in detail later)
- Printer
- Desk
- Chair (a comfy one!)
- Desk lamp
- File cabinet or cart
- Bookshelf

It's important to have all these supplies on hand in your office space. The last thing you want is to seem disorganized when talking with potential clients, and looking for a pen or having difficulty recalling a previous conversation because you can't find someone's folder or pull up the info on your computer is a sure giveaway.

Defining Your Space

Finding a location for your office has gotten easier with the invention of everything wireless; the location is now not dictated by where wires and hookups are. Here are some thoughts to ponder as you decide on your office space.

To begin with, make sure you clearly define your home office space, especially to any little entrepreneurs who might be running around. It's important to have a space that is used strictly for your business. You want it to remain somewhat private from the main area of the house. The smaller your space, of course, the trickier this gets. If you live in a one-bedroom apartment, your bedroom should be your sanctuary and off limits to the energy a new business will bring. Instead, think about dividing your other living space to create an area for work as well. If you share the living space with a spouse, children, or roommate, then you'll have to get creative. You might use room dividers or furniture to wall off some of the space, or create a schedule listing those times when you'll have exclusive use of it. Maybe all you need is a good set of headphones to help you concentrate on the tasks at hand. Just remember that privacy and quiet will be critical.

I once had a client whose home business took up a section of her living room. At first I thought this was an impossible situation, but it turned out to work like a charm. While her children were in school, my client enjoyed the light from the many windows, the convenience of the nearby kitchen, and access to the TV when she wanted it; her laundry room was close by, too, so she could multitask when necessary. When her children arrived home, she closed up shop for the day. This arrangement forced her to be efficient with the time she had alone. She completed her work (which was mostly on the phone) while her children weren't around. Then, when she had computer work or paperwork, she could do it while supervising her children as they finished their homework at the kitchen table. It was my job to help her get her space looking more presentable and organized so as to not be such an eyesore for guests.

Your office should be a space you will enjoy sitting in for some time, especially at first. You'll be on the phone with potential clients, so make sure that wherever you are, the family noise, if any, will be masked or you can close a door to shut it out completely. It's intensely frustrating to try to take a client call with cartoons or a family dispute blaring in the background. It's okay for clients to know you work from home, but their experience with you should be as productive and professional as if you were sitting in a corporate office.

Phone, Fax, and Computer

Now that you have decided on a location for your office, it's time to get wired up.

Phone Lines

Call your phone company to discuss your options. Typically a business line—which allows you to list your business in the phone book and will have the business name attached to it if anyone calls information—is more expensive than a residential line. If this is not an expense you're willing to incur right now, ask about adding a second line to your existing residential line. This option costs $30 to $60 less per month than a business line. Once you have established your business, you can turn your existing number into a business line to add your company to the phone book and information. Something to remember if you choose not to get a business line: When you call clients, their caller ID will show the name of the person who owns the account, not your business name. This isn't a big deal if the phone line is in your name, but if it's in your spouse's name or that of a roommate, you might want to change the name on the account or set up a business line.

Make sure that wherever your phone is located, any little ones in the house can't accidentally pick it up and answer when potential clients are on the line. By the same token, when the phone rings at night or early in the morning, it shouldn't disturb your home or private time. So if your office is within earshot of your bed, turn the ringer down or off during non work hours. I've had clients call at very odd hours to leave messages. If a tired spouse picked up the phone by accident, the client would instantly feel uncomfortable—and most likely would hesitate to call in the future.

In the early days of your business, if the phone rings—even in the middle of the night—you'll be too curious to resist answering it. Do yourself a favor and eliminate the temptation: No ringing business phones where you can hear them during non-work hours!

Answering Machine Versus Voice Mail

This is very important. You want quality and convenience. You don't want to use the old recycled machine that you had in your basement that sounds like you're talking from inside a tin can, or the one that makes your voice sound like a robot, as some of the new digital ones do. Go for the voice-mail service offered by your phone company. The cost is typically minimal, and the convenience and quality are unmistakable. You can easily retrieve calls when you're away from home, and your outgoing message will sound clear and professional.

Another advantage to this service is that you can have voice mail pick up phone calls when you're already on the line. I urge you to opt out of call waiting, with all its annoying beeps and clicks. Anytime you're on the phone with a client and the phone starts beeping, you will—trust me—get distracted wondering who might be calling in and lose your train of thought. It's unprofessional and unnecessary.

Outgoing Message

The message you place on your voice mail is important, too. I find that when potential clients want to talk about getting organized, they've generally thought long and hard about it before making the call—and when they do call, they're anxious to speak to a live person. I change my message daily to let callers know whether I'm in the office or not. If I'll be out, I tell people when they can expect a callback. This is just another way to show callers you are respectful of their time—it's actually a technique that I teach my time-management clients. Here is a sample message:

> Hello, you have reached Balance & Beyond. It's Tuesday, May 5th. Someone will be in the office at 2 p.m. today. Your call is very important to us. Please leave a message, and we will get back to you later today.

Try to avoid "No one is in the office." Replace that with "Someone will be in the office at . . ." or "We will be in the office . . ." The *we*, of course, makes your company sound more corporate than *I*. Even if it's just you and your gerbil, it's okay to say *we*.

For a while I switched to using a generic message, but colleagues and clients alike told me that they preferred knowing whether I was there and when I would most likely get back to them. So I went back to recording a daily message. This also assures you that your phone lines and voice mail are working. There's little worse than learning that someone's been trying to reach you—but couldn't, because there was something wrong with your line.

I recently relocated my office space in my home and thought I had reconnected all the phone lines correctly. It wasn't until about a week went by that I realized I had crossed the wires; my business line was not connected, and the tone I typically hear alerting me that there are messages was not coming through. I corrected the situation and found that several callers had been waiting for responses for days. Don't let this happen to you!

800 Numbers

Do you need an 800 number? Right now, probably not. Besides, you will be target-marketing within your local area, so your phone number will be local for most clients. An 800 number is another expense that you can avoid as you start up. Eventually, as your business grows—and especially if you're intending to sell products or work with clients outside your area—you might reconsider an 800 number. But don't worry about it yet.

Cell Phones

No two ways about it: You must have a cell phone. It is an essential business tool for the work you'll be doing. I'm going to surprise you, though, and advise you *not* to share this number with clients. As good as cell phones are, they're also unpredictable. I have found that some messages come through immediately, while others sometimes take hours. I never want clients waiting for a callback. So I always tell them to call my office number—even if I'll be out of the office—and reassure them that I check my voice mail often. If you're using a phone company voicemail, you can also select a service that forwards calls to your cell phone at any time. (Google Voice, for example, has this service available.) This practice also eliminates the need for clients to remember two different numbers.

So why have a cell phone? For several reasons. You will be on the road traveling to client homes; it sometimes becomes necessary to check directions, or to let folks know that traffic has held you up. Also, I usually make it a point to arrive early for appointments, so that I can park around the corner, check my voice mail, and return any calls that need immediate attention while I wait for my appointment time.

Fax Lines

Do you need a fax line? My new answer to this is no. I have faxed fewer and fewer items over the past years. I think I only faxed one item in the past twelve months, so I've disconnected my fax and there it sits on the shelf in the event some oldie but goodie requests something be faxed. But if you're starting out, I see no need for you to purchase one. It's just as easy now to scan something and e-mail it.

Computer

Odds are you already have a computer. If so, that's great—there's no need for you to take on the additional expense right now. If you don't have one, there are two options: Get one or don't. Either way you can still start and run your business. Many of the tasks of running an office are made easier with a computer, but the truth is that it's not essential to managing client information or doing the work you love.

That said, I highly recommend having one. If you're new to the high-tech world, taking a computer course at your local library would be a great starting point.

Of course, computer decisions don't end with *To own or not to own*. Should you get a Mac or a PC? What about a cable versus phone line versus wireless hookup? Desktop or laptop (or the newest term, *netbook*)?

Whenever you're faced with a multitude of options, a good way to approach the issue is to create a list of needs and wants, *then* take your list and go shopping!

Sample Computer Wish List

- Large screen
- Portability
- High speed
- Simple connections to ancillary hardware
- Ability to burn CDs
- Word-processing software I'm familiar with
- Operating system I'm familiar with
- Good technical support lines
- Current budget
- Wireless ancillaries (wires versus emitting radio waves)

Armed with your list, visit a local computer store or search the Internet and find the perfect computer for your needs. You will be getting recommendations for software programs throughout this book—keep a running list of the ones you're interested in and bring that with you as you search for a computer. Most computers come with software packages; you might find that the programs you need are preloaded onto your new machine.

"It's Not If, It's When"

Whatever computer system you choose, making sure you have backup scheduled on a regular basis is key to sleeping well at night. While referring to my computer crashing, my support person once said to me, "It's not if, it's when..." He said this to scare me into making sure backup was taken care of. My computer backs up to an external hard drive each night, and I exchange this hard drive with one I keep in my fire safe every month. In the event of a fire, I will always have a back up that's not more than one month old. Other ways to take care of backing up files are to use Internet services that offer offsite storage of your data. The options are endless, so there's no excuse not to backup your files. I don't care how you do it, just do it!

Creating Boundaries

So here you are working from home, making client calls in your slippers, doing a load of laundry or two when you need a break from the computer—you've got the ultimate in flexible work hours! But if you don't create boundaries for your family and friends, your business *and* personal lives may both suffer. It can be tricky to handle the neighbor who needs you to pinch-hit as a babysitter for an hour or so, or that "Since you're home I thought I'd stop by for a visit" friend. Then there's the spouse who imagines that dinner will be on the table promptly every night, "since you're home all day anyway." These situations need to be addressed as they occur, or you'll quickly find yourself running behind on your business tasks. Sure, it can be tempting to get distracted by these interruptions, especially when you're at work on a task that is less than enthralling. But don't. You need to establish boundaries with everyone in your life, letting them know that you have work that needs to get done so you can enjoy your downtime.

I've found that if I let my family know when I'll be done for the day—say, 3:30 or 4:45 p.m.— they respect my need for privacy and let me get things done. When I leave them in the dark, though, they interrupt me to get their needs met. If you have little ones in your house with a sitter or other family member, they may still want you. One way to discourage them from disturbing you is to hang a sign on your office door letting them know when they can and can't come in. A smiley face and the word YES or a quiet face and the word PRIVACY may help.

Setting boundaries is especially important when you are making phone calls to clients. Again, it's okay for your clients to know you work from home; just remember that if you're on a call with a client and your spouse walks in with a crying baby, it's not the most professional way to conduct a phone call.

Work Discipline

Don't get me wrong, working from home is wonderful, but if the nuts and bolts of running your business—the planning, the budgeting, the paperwork—aren't something you look forward to, it can suddenly become more important to put up that picture you've been meaning to hang, or to call your aunt because you haven't spoken to her in a while. It will take discipline and a written schedule to keep you on track the first few months. Once you're in a routine, you can lighten up on yourself, but in the beginning I highly recommend posting a written schedule of office hours for you and other family members to see and respect.

Monica Ricci, Catalyst Organizing Solutions, LLC

Getting started in business: Having had two businesses prior to this one—one of which "was a big failure," she says—Monica identified that she needed "a business that I loved."

Budget and finances: "Budget? What budget? I kept my part-time job for four years while I was starting the business. This financed all the start-up costs. I didn't leave it until I felt comfortable that the business was there." It should be easier these days to get started, of course, as there is more recognition among the general public of what organizers are all about and the work we can do.

Greatest challenge: Monica says, "Keeping the client pipeline full" is where she focuses her attention when she's not doing actual organizing work. She has relied on her strengths as a writer to market her business by crafting articles for websites and magazines, blogging, and serving as moderator for an organizing site.

Keeping the balance: Monica says her greatest reward is "when clients call or e-mail and tell me how their life is better because of the work we've done together. I help them remove the roadblocks, and that helps them move on with life." Monica attributes her own balance to her quiet time by herself, enlightenment books, and "good support from my husband."

Even with posted hours, I have struggled with this issue for years, and at times I still do. I'm not the only one; even if you were the soul of discipline in a corporate environment, it's disturbingly easy to get distracted when it's just you and your dog, with the sun shining in the windows and no one but yourself to hold you accountable. What I have found effective is to create tight deadlines for myself with a treat at the end. For instance, if I work up that outline for my corporate presentation by 1 p.m., I get to search the Internet for the bins for my client's office. It seems to work for me, but you will have to discover on your own what keeps you on track. Another trick is to leave Friday as a day for office work, client research and preparation, phone calls, and the like. I'm so excited to finish my work knowing the weekend is here that I seem to crank through these tasks much more quickly than if it were Monday morning.

There are many books out there on the subject of task management, and since you'll potentially be assisting clients with this, any knowledge or techniques you gain now will only add to your repertoire.

The Balancing Act

Debbie Ennis, home business owner and entrepreneur

"Learning to work from an office out of my home has been one of my greatest challenges. I have a nine-year-old daughter who reminds me ever-so-nicely that 'time together' isn't running errands to the local office store or making client calls. I had to get clear about my office hours and the hours I would spend with my daughter. I recently started renting office space in an old Victorian home down the block with other professionals. This has made balancing work and playtime much easier"

Your Business Filing System

Once you decide to go into business, information will start pouring in—catalogs, mailings, Internet downloads, reference materials, you name it. You need to get a handle on your papers immediately. Nothing will crush your confidence as an organizer more fully than a desk full of papers piled so high you can't find what you're looking for.

So how to keep track of it all? Your filing system and your computer will quickly become the backbone of your business.

A filing system is critical to keeping a business organized. I have found that paperwork is part of almost every organizing job I do. Every client, from the hotshot executive to the stay-at-home mom, has paperwork issues. You will be no exception if you don't design your filing system to suit your needs as a start-up business and entrepreneur. Getting your paperwork in order is thus not only a business-saving venture, but also a lesson learned that you can take to any client you work with.

I'll go over all the nitty-gritty details of working with clients and their paperwork in a later chapter; for now, let me give you an amazingly effective structure for your own filing system. If your current system works for you 100 percent of the time, of course, go ahead and keep it. If it doesn't, take a look at the following guidelines.

Start out with these categories:

- Clients
- Business Operations
- Marketing
- Resources/Products

Here's an example of this system in operation:

Clients

- Corporate (plastic tab)
    - ABC Company
    - Wetland Associates
- Private (plastic tab)
    - Booker, Terry
    - Moore, Linda
- Speaking Gigs Completed

Business Operations

- Banking statements
- Business plan
- Computer instructions
- DBA
- Domain name
- Phone lines
- Receipts
- Taxes
- Trademark

Marketing

- Advertising ideas/design
- Ad clippings
- Marketing opportunities
- Portfolio
- Press release info
- Speaking opportunities

Resources/Products

- Closet organizing
- Computer support
- Decorating ideas/services
- Handouts (plastic tab) filing instructions
- "How Long Do I Keep It" list
- File index blanks

Each category will have its own color. For instance, Clients folders may be in red, Business Operations in blue, Marketing in green, and Resources/Products in yellow.

The names of these categories can differ slightly, depending on what terms instinctively feel right to you; even your file names might be different. Think of these as ideas to get started.

Each category will grow as your business grows. Still, I have had the same four categories since I began my company, and they have served me well.

Filing Tips

- Use straight tab filing—that is, with all tabs either left, right, or center, not alternating. Straight tab filing is much easier on the eye, and you can add or delete files anytime without ruining your pattern.

- Keep plastic tabs to a minimum. Use them only to designate separate sections within a category, e.g., CORPORATE and PRIVATE in the client category.

- File folder label should be all-capital letters, black ink on white labels.

- Always buy the best-quality file folders.

- See "Start-Up Costs" in chapter 1.

- Each file category should be stored in its own drawer.

Client Database Management

Managing client information is crucial—and without a system, it will get out of hand quickly. Even if you think you have a mind like a steel trap, I'm here to tell you that remembering names, conversations, where you met someone, and more will become overwhelming.

When I was a new business owner, I went to many networking meetings, leaving each time with a handful of business cards. After several similar meetings I found myself with more than a hundred business cards. Remembering my conversations with many of these people was impossible. From desperation, I created my contact-management system. As soon as I left any networking meeting, I would sit in my car and write directly on each business card any information I had obtained from my conversation—whatever might help me recall the discussion and potential follow-up actions. After that, it was just a matter of getting this information into my computer database and scheduling follow-up phone calls and other tasks. When I ran out of free time to do this myself, I hired a high school student to help input everything.

There are many database-management products out there. The three that stand out are ACT! (www.act.com; this is the one I use), QuickBooks Customer Manager (http://quickbooks.intuit.com), and Contact Plus Professional (www.contactplus .com). A check of the Internet will show what these products offer and how they are laid out. It's worth finding out whether the software you're considering offers a free trial—something I highly recommend. Also, call the company's service line to learn how quick it is when it comes to customer support. All these little things will become very important when you're in business and trying to get things done. If you have friends in a business that requires client information management, ask for their opinions, too—remembering that what works for them won't necessarily work for you.

The database you choose should be able to search for client records by name (first or last), city, town, company, and even where you met. What this means is that if someone calls you and says, "It's Betty from MRG," and you have no recollection of her, you can quickly search either "Betty" or "MRG" in your database. Either will allow you to immediately access all of Betty's information, including your last conversations with her. What else can you use your database for? It allows you to create e-mail campaigns; lets you schedule follow-up phone calls with alarm features;

What Goes into Your Client Database?

The information you will be capturing on your database typically includes the following:

For Individual or Private Clients

Name

Phone number

Alternate phone number

Address

E-mail

Children's names

Spouse's name

Reason for initial call

Ongoing conversations

Approval to be on mailing list

For Corporate Clients

Name of company

Name of contact

Title of contact

Address of company

Phone number

Web address

E-mail

Fax

Reason for initial call

Ongoing conversations

Approval to be on mailing list

offers word-processing features that let you write form letters addressed to specific clients; synchronizes information with other software programs or your PDA or smart phone; and helps you set up a calendar or schedule. At this writing all three programs run around $200, give or take.

Connecting with Contacts

We'll discuss marketing in more detail later in the book. However, finding a good resource to help with e-mailing newsletters, special offers, and general 'keeping in touch' notes is helpful and it would be nice if the database you chose played well with your e-mail support. The ones I have found easy to work with include Constant Contact, Vertical Response, and Get Response. It's worth a glance at these services while in the process of choosing your contact database software.

In addition to my computer database for contacts and clients, I also keep hard-copy client folders that I can take along with me on each client visit. This is where I record the work that we have done, our schedule of visits, and what we are planning to work on next. I don't transfer this information into my database; it just seems like too much work to me. So my computer database is for conversations, new contacts, and prospects. Once these potential clients become real ones, I keep records of all the work we do in their folder.

The Look

Creating the look for your company is exciting. If you've been thinking about going into business for yourself for a while now, you may have some ideas. If not, it may be time to get creative! Either way, you'll want a look that you love. It will be used for all correspondence and any forms or materials you use for clients.

So do you need a logo or will it suffice to have the name of the company at the top of your letterhead? Should you create something on your own computer, or is it wiser to work with a professional? The answers depend on both your budget and your creative talents. Some people just use the name of their company as a design element and forgo a logo; it's up to you. I sat and doodled variations on my company name for hours, trying to coming up with something I liked. Interestingly, the answer finally hit me in my sleep. One morning I awoke with an idea in mind of how my logo would look. I went to a family member who happened to be the art director and owner of his own ad agency and asked if he could work with me to create something. Much to my surprise, an hour after we sat down together in front of

Advice Worth Repeating!

It's not "if" my computer crashes, it's "when." Backing up your computer files is essential. If you're not sure how to backup your files, contact a computer support person who can walk you through the process. You can also find software programs that run backup and virus checks at regular, preprogrammed times. It doesn't matter how it gets done as long as it gets done.

I worked with a client once who ran a business out of her home. As we reviewed her electronic client files, I asked when she'd last backed up her computer.

"Backed up?" she said.

Well, I stopped everything right there and told her I wouldn't proceed until she had all her files safe. She was amazed at how simple the process was and grateful to have it completed.

Your own files are just as critical. Think, too, about how you'll store your backups. I know a family who once lost everything they owned in a house fire. Luckily no one was hurt, but all of the family business records were destroyed, despite being stored in metal file cabinets. After watching everything these friends went through to reestablish their business, I purchased a fireproof box that I keep in my basement. This contains CD copies of all my computer information, both business and personal, along with other important papers.

the computer and I told him what I had envisioned, the logo came to life. Between my ideas and his creative abilities, we created the logo that I continue to use today.

Choosing my company colors was also fun. We printed about ten two-color variations on the logo on a single page. I carried it around with me, and every chance I got I asked friends or family which one they liked. What I found, though, was that each time I pulled out the page, my own eye was attracted to the same two choices. Interestingly, everyone else who viewed the options also picked out one of my two favorites! I finally settled on one of them, and my logo was born.

Then came the reality check. I was so excited to have a design that I didn't realize what it would cost me. Custom two-color business cards, letterhead, envelopes, and stationery were definitely out of my budget at the time. The printer informed me that a black-and-white version of my logo would bring the cost down considerably. Then I asked myself: *Do I really need letterhead and envelopes?* I hadn't used either one yet, and I was two months into operations. What I really needed, I realized, was business cards and forms to use when I went to work with clients.

Convinced that business cards were essential, I splurged on getting those printed in my exact color scheme. But since I now had a version of my logo in black and white, too, I was able to print out all my forms on my own computer, logo and all. Bingo: I had exactly what I needed, within my budget.

Home Away from Home

Even though you'll be working out of your home, you may want to consider getting an off-site address. When you advertise or hand out business cards, you probably won't want to list your home address for all to see. A company such as Mail Boxes, Etc., can provide you with a normal-looking street address. If having a post office box doesn't bother you (some folks consider a P.O. address a signal that a company has something to hide), it's inexpensive to rent one.

The Brochure

Next up came my brochure. I sat for hours in my basement office designing, redesigning, and re-redesigning a brochure that I hoped would cover every question ever asked about what my business had to offer. It never seemed right, though, and I continued to change it ad infinitum. Finally I realized that I needed some coaching in this area and asked my printer for suggestions.

After an hourlong meeting, we settled on a single card piece about 3.5 by 8.5 inches. This design forced me to stop going on and on about my services: I had to be concise and direct. With the help of one of their designers, I came up with a look that was simple, clean, and impactful. I loved the fact that it was a bit different, and with its smaller size I could have it printed in color. I love the piece to this day, and it's needed only a few minor changes through the years.

Still, the most important lesson I've learned about my brochure is that most of the people who are interested in my services can't find it anyway—they already have too much paper to deal with! As you work on your own similar pieces, then, I urge you to think simple, think different, think outside the box. Take advantage of the Internet; if clients would like more information, they can always look to your website (a topic I'll cover in detail shortly). I also have printed out pages from my website to send to anyone interested in my services who did not have access to the Internet. The Internet can be especially useful with regard to rates, which are subject to change. Scrapping printed materials and reprinting each time your fees change wastes time and money.

Bottom line on the brochure? Think two or three times, and maybe even four, before you take the plunge. Do you really need it, or would your time and money be better spent elsewhere—say, on a website?

Organizer, Heal Thyself

As an organizer, any materials you use must be simple and easy for clients to use. And remember that in this business, you are always interviewing potential clients. If your materials are hard to understand, or seem disorganized, that's a bad signal to send out. This applies to your website as much as to every aspect of your professional presentation.

Website Development

So when and how do you decide if you need to be present on the web? That original brochure of mine was so full of information, it was like picking up a card in the card store that has too much writing on it—you sometimes just put it back down before you even finish reading. People are so busy these days, they want the answers to their questions as quickly as possible! My website, on the other hand, turned out to be a great tool for providing clients with additional information. Some people want to see before-and-after pictures—they want to be inspired. Others want to know more about you, the organizer, and still others are strictly interested in "How much will this cost me?" Fitting all this information into a brochure is an overwhelming task; not so on the web.

Good, Better, Best Website Design

Good: Use software such as Dreamweaver from Adobe to design your own website.
Better: Find a company that offers templates for websites and takes you through the steps toward designing your own. Two such sites are www.buildyoursite.com and www.homestead.com. A visit to www.Intuit.com will provide you with a robust website builder and a variety of small business ad ons that are very helpful.
Best: Go to a service like www.sleeklogos.com and have them work their magic for you quickly, affordably, and beautifully, and save your energy for something else. Check out my site (www.balanceandbeyond.com) and see for yourself!

There is, of course, a cost to this. It could be time, if you are inclined to build and maintain your own site, or it could come in the form of paying someone to do the work for you. I decided to learn how to build my own site using a particular software, which is not something I would recommend these days. Rather I suggest you work with an online services that provides you with templates, and other easy-to-use tools, to click and build You can always choose to hire someone, which can be a bit pricey, but you'll get a customized look and be able to work directly with the person designing your site. If cost is an issue, there's always the route of trading services. Along the way to creating my company, I found many other individuals who were doing the same. Working with a web designer who needs help organizing can provide both of you with an opportunity for before-and-afters, cut down on money needed to get your business started, and get you onto the web.

Where do you start when it comes to designing or telling your designer what you want your site to look like or contain? Well, that's just a click away. Take a tour of other websites (especially other organizers' sites) and keep a running list of your likes and dislikes. Keep a list of the "tabs" or pages you'd like on your site. Label a sheet of paper with the tab or page—say, "About Us," "Our Services," or "Contact Us"—and begin jotting down everything you want to include on that page. It doesn't have to be in any particular order or even make sense right now; you're just brainstorming. This is a great way to begin the design process. Also, if you're working with a good designer, the designer will give you guidance in this area.

The site should reflect your personality and the energy and feel of your company. Is it business lite? Casual? Fun? Be careful, though: I have seen websites that are riddled with advertisements and things flashing and moving. When potential clients come to your site, they are looking to see if you can help them create calm amid their chaos. If your website looks like Disney World at spring break, it's unlikely to communicate that feeling of calm.

Having a website these days is critical in my opinion. It's a tool allowing clients and potential clients a glimpse of what you can do to make their lives better. Use it wisely. Keep it simple, and remember the organizer's mantra: Less is more.

Find Your Unique Web Philosophy

There are as many different approaches to websites as there are, well, websites. Yours can be strictly informational, just as a brochure would be, detailing your services, philosophy, rates, and more. Or it can be more interactive, with potential moneymaking features such as product sales, newsletters, blogs, forums, affiliate programs, and the like. You will be introduced to the many options available throughout this book. Keep in mind that your site is very flexible: It can and will grow with you as your business grows. Start simple and specific now, and build as you go along.

03

Setting Up Your Business

Much of organizing has to do with the creating and maintaining of systems. Laying the ground work for your business is no different. The stronger your systems are for managing the legal and financial underpinnings of your business, the less likely you are to run into problems in the future. If when you evaluated your skills for being a business owner you were lacking in any key business areas, I recommend that as you read through this chapter, you jot down your thoughts and questions along the way. Then create a plan for yourself to get any problematic areas addressed. If you need to reach out to an accountant, attorney, colleague, family member, or knowledgeable friend, now is the time to be diligent about getting your ducks in a row.

Moving forward with your business before the financial and legal pieces are securely in place will impede your progress: For example, if you can't receive a check in your business name because you haven't set up a bank account, this could send a red flag to your customer that you are not as organized as you advertise and undermine your professional image. Also, if you haven't taken all the necessary steps to formalize your business structure with your town or county and you find out after you've printed 500 business cards that there is another company with an identical name...well you get the picture. It could be costly and time consuming to fix something that could have been taken care of quickly and efficiently right from the start.

Naming Your Business

There is so much fun and satisfaction in naming your company. There are many different theories about naming a business. Some say your business name should announce what it is you do; others believe the most important thing is a name that's unique and memorable.

No matter what approach you take, the name of the business will be an integral part of your marketing effort. If you aren't completely satisfied with the name, you'll encounter problems each step of the way, from creating your logo and business cards to designing ads and brochures. Take your time and try out several different names with family and friends. Ultimately, however, you need to go with what feels right for you and your new venture.

Here are some questions to ponder while coming up with a name. Remember, they are just guidelines. Use them to challenge and confirm the name you already have, or to help you arrive at the perfect moniker:

- What is the image you want to project?
- Can you create a logo around it?
- How does it sound when you answer the phone?
- How does it sound in headlines?
- Does it tell people what you do?
- Is it memorable?
- Is it short and easy to remember?
- Is it appropriate for your target market?
- Is it available with a .com extension?
- Might it leave people confused as to what you do?
- Google it and see what comes up—is it good or bad?
- Is it easy to create a tagline around it, or does it go with your tagline? (You don't necessarily need a tagline, but it seems to add a bit to the name when you include it in some forms of advertising. My own business, for instance, is known as "Balance & Beyond: Inspiration for Better Living." I think this tells people a little more about what we do.)
- Create draft business cards and letterhead. Does it look good?
- Do you love it?

It's also wise to get other people's opinions. Show your potential new name to family and friends, or try it out on a few strangers. What do they think? Does the name tell them what it is you do? Do they believe it would be easy to remember?

After answering the question *Do I love it?*, the two most important things to do about your business name are to see if it's already being used and to obtain the .com.

So how do you find whether the name is being used? Begin by checking locally. Your city or county has a record of all businesses that have been registered and will not allow you to register a similar name for a similar business. To find out what is required to register the name with your state, visit www.sba.gov and look for your particular state. Most often, however, the process is handled on a local level—you simply take a trip to your local city hall or county office, fill out a form, pay a fee, and you're done. Most states require you to report any name you are doing business under if it's not your proper name; this fictitious or assumed business name is also known as your DBA or Doing Business As.

If you're going to do business outside your local area, whether statewide or nationwide, you'll need to either record your name in all those other areas or trademark it (which gives you proprietary rights to it). Otherwise, someone in Alabama who has registered the same name and trademarked it could potentially sue you—even if you live in New Jersey—if you try to use the name nationally.

I know what I'm talking about from personal experience. When I registered the name of my business, it was on the county level; there were no other businesses with that name in my county or state. This was fine for me in the beginning, but as my company grew and I had thoughts of opening additional offices and doing business in other states, I searched nationally and found there exists a company with a similar name doing something similar to what I do. I have not at this time been allowed to trademark my company name. My recommendation is that you check it both locally and nationally at the same time. If it's not being used nationally, then, in addition to registering it for business use locally, trademark it as well. The current cost to trademark a name is approximately $375. If you hire an attorney to help, the fee is typically between $800 and $1,500. There are attorneys who specialize in this process, and they can do the job for you quickly and efficiently. If you have the patience and time, though, it's something you can certainly handle on your own.

These fees may seem steep now, but if anyone comes along who wants to use your business name in any area you currently do business in, they can serve you with a cease-and-desist order. You'd then have to change the name of your company immediately, making your printed material or websites useless. Save yourself the potential heartache and trademark it now.

Creating a Business Entity

The term *business entity* refers to your business structure or, for lack of a better description, how you report your business legally to the state and federal government. You need to do this in order to set up your business banking accounts.

Consulting with a lawyer or tax accountant may be useful to you. The following is a description of the different types of legal structures and how they compare. When deciding which type of structure to follow, keep these three factors in mind: simplicity, tax implications, and personal risk or liability.

Sole Proprietorship

Of all the legal structures, this one is certainly the easiest: Setting one up requires very little paperwork. The vast majority of small businesses start out this way, then grow from there.

Sole proprietors have complete control over the day-to-day operation of their business, including the finances. You don't draw a salary, but you can take funds from the business at any time. Also, any funds you need to keep the business running come from your personal accounts or personal loans. You file your taxes just as you would file a personal return—with the addition of Form 1040, Schedule C, which integrates your business with your personal return.

The downside is that liability for debts is considered your personal liability—your house, car, bank accounts, and so forth are all at risk. Typically, though, you won't encounter any real liability threats as you start up your organizing business, and your overhead is extremely low. Thus this business structure is usually sufficient for the fledgling business owner. Even if you have now or plan to have employees, you can still be considered a sole proprietor.

Partnership

A partnership is appropriate when two or more people intend to run a business together. It's set up very similarly to a sole proprietorship, except that *both* parties are now legally responsible for the actions of the other. These agreements can be verbal, but I highly recommend using a written agreement that has been reviewed by an attorney. This agreement should cover how the partners share responsibility, how the profits and losses are distributed, and how liabilities are dealt with, as well as how prolonged illnesses, disability, or death would affect the partnership. You should also consider what would happen if a partner wanted out, for whatever reason. This agreement can be revised or amended at any time—and it should be if there are any major changes in how business is conducted.

The benefits of partnerships are many: You have someone with whom you can share expenses including computer software, office equipment, marketing, and more. You also have someone to share the workload and any losses; it's nice to have another creative mind to work with to continue growing the business; and you have someone to fill your shoes when you're on vacation or unexpectedly have to take the dog to the vet.

Filing for taxes is done just as for a sole proprietor—the forms used are Form 1065 which is filed for the company and you, as a partner receive the K1 to be filed with your personal taxes—but following your partnership agreement, whether that specifies a 50–50 split of profit and loss, a 30–70 split, or any other combination. All these details should be determined up front and included in your contract.

Corporation

Corporations are considered a separate entity from the owners. It is the corporation that is liable for damages, the corporation that can be sued and taxed, not the individual. The shareholders are the owners of a corporation.

It's my belief this type of business entity is not a place to start your new venture. If your business is growing at such a pace that you have many employees and are looking for funding from major sources, you need to contact an attorney and tax accountant for professional guidance in this area.

Limited Liability Company (LLC)

This is very similar to a partnership, but more structured. You will have to write up a business agreement, and there are requirements in the form of meetings and filings with the state. You'll enjoy the limited liability of a corporation, but the tax flexibilities of a partnership.

When my sister and I decided to join forces in business several years after I'd started as a sole proprietor, we wanted something a bit more structured than a partnership, but without the intensity and hassle of a corporation. We chose the LLC as the ideal form for our efforts. We have since dissolved the LLC, as she has spun off into her own business as a separate entity (she does mostly behavioral training and education, which, combined with my side of the business, was getting too confusing for visitors to my site). I can share with you that I much prefer being a sole proprietor status as the tax and accounting components are much simpler.

A new version of LLC is the Sole Member LLC, which gives you the protection of an LLC, but the benefits of remaining a sole proprietor. Ask your accountant about this type of LLC; it may be the best answer for you.

Scary, Intimidating and How, LLC, Accounting Firm

Ok, so here's a bit of self-disclosure: I've never been good about maintaining the finances of my business. My first visit to an accountant to ask all the questions I had about setting up my business was a disaster. It was two hours of conversation that was less than helpful, and was more about him trying to talk me out of starting my business; I left frustrated and with few answers. It got worse: Several days later I received a bill from the accountant in the mail for $500! Yes, he charged me $250 an hour to chat. From that point on I decided I would handle finances myself, which has caused me some stress. For the life of my business I have forever struggled with every aspect of tracking and managing the finances.

Fast forward several years and I finally have the nerve to talk with an accountant who is part of a firm. I had always thought I wasn't a big enough business to work with a firm, and so I never met with one. What I've come to understand, however, is that accounting firms work with all sizes of businesses, from small scale sole proprietors all the way up to large corporations, and of all revenue levels. They work closely with you setting up a relationship that fits your budget and makes sense for your business. The accountants become your "partners" in making sure the financial well-being of your company is on course.

I highly recommend you interview several accountants and accounting firms to help you with your company's finances and find one that you feel would be a good partner for this purpose.

When calling to set up this consultation, ask these questions first: Does the firm/accountant charge for the consultation? Does the firm/accountant work with small businesses? If the answers are no and yes, then set up a "free" consultation to get to know the firm/accountant and take it from there.

Insurance Needs

When I started my business, I couldn't imagine I'd need insurance. *I'll be moving plastic containers around, I figured, organizing basements, cleaning out playrooms. What in the world would I need insurance for?* Then, early on, I began working with clients who were having an addition built, which involved a decorator, contractor, builder, and other subcontractors. Sometime during the build the clients had carpet installed. The carpet person inadvertently used tacks that were the wrong length, puncturing the floor heating system that ran throughout this family room. No one was the wiser until several weeks later the garage (which, by the way, was completely organized with built-in closets) sprouted mold all over the walls and cabinets. Apparently the floor heating system had been leaking for weeks due to the tack punctures. A lawsuit ensued against everyone involved in the addition—the contractor, because he'd brought in the decorator; the decorator, because she'd hired the carpet person; and so on down the line.

As I watched the saga unfold, I realized that professional organizers make suggestions about furniture placement and product use; we even get involved in moving things around. All the what-ifs started coming to my mind: *What if I help move a piece of furniture and it scratches the floor? What if that piece of furniture falls after I leave?* Well, having insurance could ease your mind.

I do my best to ensure that everything I do is safe, of course. If I have any concerns about something, I don't do it and recommend the client get assistance from a handyman, spouse, or family friend. That being said, I also carry insurance and hope I never have to use it. As my company grew, it was easy to upgrade my coverage to encompass the organizers out there working for me.

So liability insurance should be first on your list. If you are planning to join one of the associations for professional organizers, you can find out more from them about liability insurance. Most associations work exclusively with a single provider, giving expertise and possibly a discount on rates right there. If not, speak with a local insurance agent whom you feel comfortable with and who is familiar with business liability insurance.

What other types of insurance might you need? If you are working from home and self-employed, think about the following:

- Fire and general property insurance
- Life insurance
- Health insurance
- Business-interruption or disability insurance
- Errors and omissions insurance
- Car insurance (additional coverage may be necessary if you're using your vehicle for business)
- Workers' compensation

You certainly don't need all this insurance at once, or at all in some cases. Instead, you can obtain these various types of coverage as you grow and they are called for. For instance, if you have health insurance through a part-time job or a spouse, you don't need it at this time. Still, before you make any rash decisions to leave a job that offers health coverage, get rate quotes so you know what to expect should you choose to get coverage as a small business. As your company grows, be sure to update your policies to cover additional employees, equipment, and any new business practices.

What About Business Property Insurance?

Some homeowners' or rental insurance policies require additional coverage if you are operating a business from your home. This would be especially pertinent if you intend to carry stock of any supplies or products. Also, you want to ensure that all your business equipment—computer, fax machine, and so on—will be covered in the event of loss.

Bonding

I have never been asked if I'm bonded, but you should be aware of the term. To be *bonded* means that you are capable of paying any claim immediately. If there were extensive damage to a client's property, for instance, and a claim ensued, you can guarantee payment if you're bonded. How? By paying a bonding company. This company will settle the claim; you are then responsible for reimbursing the company. This is very different from insurance.

You may be asked about bonding when you work for a corporate client. I advise that you not get bonded (with all its expense) before you need to be—but it's also wise to be ready for bonding at any time. A bonding agency will require a background check on you and any employees or subcontractors doing work for you—so simply have these done yourself. Then, when your corporate client asks if you are bonded, you would reply, "No, but we are capable and will comply if you request."

Financial Matters

Setting up your financial records is critically important to your sanity as well as the success of your business. Your bookkeeping system doesn't have to be complex—it could be as simple as a box on your desk and a trip to the accountant—but it must be efficient and comprehensive. You can be as involved or uninvolved as you'd like.

There are so many intricacies when it comes to your finances, you could spend the next two years learning everything you need to know about the tax and accounting world. But why? You're an organizer because this is the work you love, and the same holds true when it comes to money: Do what you love. If you love tossing your receipts in a container and being done with it, great. If you're interested in learning about the new deduction or tax form for the year, then by all means do so.

Whatever your preference, the following section will provide you with some great resources for you to sink your teeth into. Let's get started.

Setting Up Bank Accounts

Armed with your license or registration certificate, go to the local bank of your choice and establish your business bank account. Find out if it offers online services (most do these days) and ask about the specific monthly administration fees.

I set up my business account at the same bank where I held my personal account. I asked if, as a new start-up, I could get a break on my business-account monthly fees. I was offered the account free of charge for a year before the standard $19.95 monthly fee kicked in. That was a savings of almost $240! It pays to ask.

Also ask your bank if it offers what's called a merchant account, which allows you to accept credit cards from clients. There are definitely costs involved in this for you, but it makes it easier for your clients to pay. I did not have this type of an account for my first three years in business; all my clients paid by cash or check, which worked for me. But I have noticed that clients enjoy the flexibility of being able to use a credit card, especially when it comes to my larger service packages. It's worth your while to find out now if your bank offers merchant accounts, as well as how to set one up and how long it takes. This may not be something you want to do right now, but it's nice to know it's available when you're ready.

When it comes to ordering checks, through either your bank or another source, use a checking system that is easy for you. When I opened my account, I was offered one of those big check registers that sits on the desk and has little receipt tabs. I almost got it, because I remember my dad using one at the dining room table. But it would never have worked for me—I need to have my checkbook in my purse when I'm out buying products. I also need checks that come with their own duplicate copies; I'm not, unfortunately, always consistent about recording checks, and this duplicate system lets me to do it at the end of the day.

The use of checks has become somewhat obsolete with the invention of the check or debit card. It's your ATM card on steroids. You just swipe it like a credit card, and the money is immediately deducted from your checking account. If you haven't seen or used this technology, I highly recommend it. The biggest concern

A Word from the Wise(r)

My first year in business was an eye-opener. I was operating as a sole proprietor, and I had to complete my business taxes first so that they could be reflected on my personal taxes. When I went to gather my information, I realized what a mess I had on my hands. I had started doing business in April of that year, and I had no system in place for managing my expenses, payments from clients—nothing. I had saved some receipts, some deposit slips, most bank statements…what a mess! There were many transactions I never even recorded in my check register. When my husband asked me, "How much did you spend on advertising this year?" I longed to answer him. But I couldn't, because my financial records were so shoddy.

So I got one of those fancy accounting pads with all the columns and rows and started filling in by hand all the information I had in front of me. I created categories for the various receipts and kept a separate page for each month. I also listed all my deposits as well as where the money had come from—a client, a workshop, funds from my personal account, whatever. It was a fun process and I enjoyed the end result: I was able to tell my husband what I had spent not only on advertising, but also on postage, gas, office supplies, capital purchases, and more. What an enlightening exercise!

Little did I know that if I had purchased a software accounting program, I could have easily been tracking this from the beginning without taking the time to write it all in by hand. Still, the process was so encouraging, I decided to learn more about it. Ultimately I created a system that was easy for me to maintain.

with this type of payment—which, by the way, you can use just like a credit card on the Internet, over the phone, or in person—is that if you forget to keep track of your purchases either in writing or online, it's easy to get carried away. Even if you think you'll remember all the times you used your card, there's inevitably a swipe or two that you forget—especially in the beginning, when you're making so many purchases. You run the risk of bouncing a check or check card purchase if you're not watching. Trust me on that one! So if you're going the debit card route, get yourself set up to be able to view your account online whenever you like. You can also pay vendors and bills through an online account.

Maintaining the Books

Managing your money has two distinct facets: maintaining the books and preparing for taxes. Maintaining the books is the everyday capturing and recording of money going out and money coming in. Preparing for taxes is the summation of your financial information for the year tied up with a pretty bow and submitted on various forms to the IRS.

I knew from the start that I wasn't interested in either one of these tasks. Still, I certainly wanted to know how much money I was making, and I realized that I liked to know where the money was being spent as well. But the actual task of recording it seemed far too tedious for me; I was sure my time would be better spent elsewhere.

We'll talk about preparing for taxes in this book's next section; for now, let's focus on maintaining the books. There are two steps here. First: Design a system to capture all the information you need easily and effortlessly. And second: Find a good bookkeeper.

Every time I make a deposit, I write directly on the deposit receipt where the money came from. This deposit receipt then goes into a very pretty can on my desk, one that I found in a secondhand store and always wanted to use. For me it's all about the can. I love it so much I find pleasure in using it for such an important purpose. (Keep these techniques in mind for when you are working with clients. If you make staying organized fun, they will do it!) In addition, all of my receipts for purchases—whether they are for office supplies, client products, gas, tolls, or whatever—go into this can. On each receipt I write either a *C*, for "client," and the client's name, or a *B*, for "business." I also consistently use my debit card for business operating expenses and a business credit card for client purchases. These records, too, go in the can.

What I end up with is a can full of receipts, deposit slips, statements, invoices, and more. From the moment I first tried this system, I loved it—and it instantly eliminated the mess I'd created. My bookkeeper loved it because she could just grab the contents of the can and go do her thing.

What if you prefer to manage your own money and get a kick out of those accounting pads with all the fancy columns and lines? Then by all means set up your own system and run it yourself. More power to you! If you prefer, there are also many bookkeeping software packages out there, the most popular and universal being QuickBooks (http://quickbooks.intuit.com). Take a tour of this product online and determine which one best suits your needs and is easiest for you to understand. Maintaining your own books is simple if you have the knowledge and the right tools. If you're willing to take the time to learn new software, or have previous experience with it, you can be up and running with your finances in no time. You can also have someone come in and help you set these programs up and give you the nuts and bolts to get you moving. If you're working with an accountant or accounting firm, the firm/accountant will often help you get set up and may offer additional training that is specific to your needs. One advantage of the software is that at any moment, you can get a full picture of where you are financially. This is great for making decisions about marketing and other larger expenses. Also, if you're doing your banking online, the software allows you to bring that information right over into your records and incorporate it with ease. But there are disadvantages: If you haven't backed your computer up and/or you have computer problems, you could lose everything. Also, as user friendly as these programs are, they still take time to learn.

The Employer Identification Number

The Employer Identification Number or EIN (sometimes referred to as a tax ID number) is assigned by the IRS. You will need this number if you are incorporated or pay wages to one or more employees. If you are a sole proprietor with no employees, you can use your Social Security number in place of an EIN if you choose. To obtain an EIN number, go to www.irs.gov/businesses/small.

Another great website that addresses the start-up needs of businesses is www.tax.gov/calendar/resources.htm.

Preparing for Taxes

Tax preparation is a matter of summarizing your finances for the year. Still...what you have to do with that summation is a bit tricky. First, let's talk about all the different taxes you'll be responsible for and some of the bigger deductions you'll be able to claim, and then we'll check back in.

Income Tax—Quarterly Estimated Taxes

Because you are self-employed and receiving payment from clients, no one is withholding taxes from your income. You will owe income tax on this at the end of the year. However, Uncle Sam doesn't want to wait until then; he would like his money now—it's called the "pay as you go" tax.

If you expect that you will owe $1,000 or more in income tax by the end of the year, you will need to make estimated quarterly tax payments. You can calculate what your estimated taxes will be using Form 1040-ES and referring to IRS Publication 505, *Tax Withholding and Estimated Tax*. Now, I must warn you, this information packet is sixty-seven pages in length. This is one of those times that contacting an accountant may pay off as time and fees well spent! Quarterly taxes are due on the fifteenth of April, June, September, and January. There are, of course, penalties if

Friendship, Finances...Fabulous!

Catherine Powers and Kelly Ruymen are accountants *and friends* from the accounting firm Malesardi, Quackenbush, Swift & Company LLC in Englewood, New Jersey. They are as passionate about accounting and finances as you are about organizing and building your business. They say, "As you build your business, you'll want to work with an accountant or firm that you are comfortable with and trust. The ability to ask all your questions, get support when you need it and know that your finances are in good hands allows you to get on with the business that you love. You'll be working with your accountant for the life of your business, so if your first meeting with an accountant does not feel like a great fit, like you can build a good business friendship, look elsewhere, as there are accountants out there willing to work with you to make your business successful." Check out Kelly and Catherine at www.mqscpa.com.

you don't comply with the IRS standards. I'll talk in a bit about how to minimize your tax burden with your deductions.

Self-Employment Tax

Not only do you pay income tax on money earned, but also you must pay Social Security and Medicare taxes. If you believe your income will be more than $400, you will use Form 1040, Schedule SE, to calculate your self-employment tax. It is 15.3 percent of your income up to $94,200. This will be paid at tax time.

Sales Tax

If you plan to sell products that you have developed or resell products that you have in stock or have purchased on behalf of a client, you will need to calculate, collect, report, and pay sales tax to the IRS. The first step is to obtain a resale certificate. In most states this is very easy: Get on the Internet and search "resale certificate Florida" (or whatever state you live in). This will bring up the appropriate form. Just follow the instructions, and you'll usually have your certificate within days. That's the easy part. Figuring how to calculate sales tax and keeping records are a bit more involved. I'll tell you more about this in chapter 7, on product sales.

Employees and Taxes

If and when you choose to grow your business, you should be aware of the taxes associated with hiring employees. There are several: withholding (FIT), FICA, and FUTA. These are for income taxes, Medicare, Social Security, and unemployment. When you hire people, they fill out a W-4 form and claim a certain number of withholding allowances, or exemptions. Based on these exemptions and percentages for each tax, you withhold those amounts from employees' paycheck and pay them to the government. Another tax task related to employees is the W-2 form at the end of the year. W-2 summarizes the employee's income and withholding for the year. Employees must receive a copy of this by January 31; a copy must be sent to the IRS as well.

●   ●   ●

Now that you are aware of some of the taxes you will be dealing with as a business owner, let's now discuss ways in which you can retain as much of your income as possible.

Deductions

Deductions are expenses that you incur in the course of doing business that you can subtract from your total income to alleviate your tax burden. When you are a start-up company, there are many items, big and small, that you will be spending money on. It's a good idea to get familiar with what is deductible and what isn't. Still, my guess is that life is moving at breakneck speed for you right now. Thus the best way to make sure you are getting the most for your deductions is to keep *everything* and sort it out at the end.

Tax Time

"The journey through the maze of tax rules governing the self-employed, whom I call indies, must be sure footed. My role is part accountant, part guide, and part teacher. My method, which I call the Most Simple System, makes recordkeeping for indies quick and easy. With "Self-employed Tax Solutions" you will learn the basics and be on firm footing as you move forward in your independent endeavor." June Walker author of *Self-employed Tax Solutions,* www.JuneWalkerOnline.com.

Business Use of Your Home

As a home-based business, you will be allowed to deduct a variety of expenses for tax purposes. In the past conventional wisdom said that if you claimed a home office, you were more likely to get audited. Times have changed, however. There are millions of self-employed, home-based entrepreneurs out there these days, and your chances of an audit are considered no greater than those of the general public. That being said, you never want to over deduct or pad your numbers. You want to honestly report what it is you are doing, and your record keeping will need to support the numbers. I'll talk extensively about record keeping shortly. For now, let's discuss some of the ins and outs of the home office deduction.

To be considered sufficient for a deduction, a home office must meet the following criteria:

- The office must be a room or part of the home that is used *exclusively* and *regularly* for the business.
- The home must be your principal place of business.
- The home must be where you meet or deal with clients in the normal course of business. (Even if you're not meeting clients regularly in your home, if you do meet with one, it could potentially take place in your home office.)

For these purposes, the term *home* can refer to a house, condominium, apartment, or even detached property, such as a barn or garage. Anything related to the business portion of your house can be deducted. If you painted your office, for instance, you can deduct the entire cost. If you put a new roof on your house, only a percentage of it could be deducted.

There are two methods you can use to calculate what percentage of your home expenses you can deduct: area and number of rooms. If you have 1,000 square feet of living space and your office is 100 square feet, for example, then 10 percent of the cost of the roof (or any other home expenses) would be deductible. Or if you have ten rooms in the house and use two of them exclusively for business, then you can deduct 20 percent of the roof. You use your allowable percentage to calculate how much of your utilities, real estate taxes, mortgage interest, insurance premiums, depreciation, and other home expenses can be deducted as business expenses.

Form 8829, Expenses for Business Use of Your Home, is used to report this. Review this form and the instructions for completing it. Also, consulting your accountant would be helpful at this point. The accountant will be up to the minute on all the changes in the tax laws and can save you lots of time and potentially even cash!

Bookkeeping Software

Depending on how you establish your business entity, you will need to match your software to it. TurboTax Home & Business will be suitable for sole proprietors, whereas TurboTax Business will be needed for an LLC. The websites www.intuit.com and www.taxcut.com offer popular programs for managing your small business financials.

Vehicle Expenses

Another tax-time biggie is your vehicle expenses. There are two ways to deduct these costs, and you may need to compare their outcomes to determine which one would be better for you:

- **Method 1:** The number of business miles on your car times the rate at the time you are filing. The IRS or your tax preparer will know the current rate, which changes annually.
- **Method 2:** The actual vehicle expense and depreciation. To use this method, you must keep thorough records of your mileage, gas, maintenance, repairs, tolls, parking fees, ferry fees, and any towing charges, in addition to the car's depreciation.

Let's say you have a total of 18,500 miles on your car: 11,125 of them for your business and 7,375 for personal use. To calculate using the standard deduction (Method 1), simply multiply your business miles (11,125) by the standard deduction. At the time of this writing, that deduction is 37 cents, which gives you a final calculation of 11,125 x 0.37 = $4,116. This is your deduction.

To calculate your deduction using actual expenses (Method 2), divide your business miles (11,125) by your total miles to get a percentage. In our example, 11,125 ÷ 18,500 = 0.60, or 60 percent. You can now deduct 60 percent of your total vehicle

Sample Mileage Log

Date	Destination/Purpose	Starting Mileage	Ending Mileage	Total
2/23/04	Joe Rocker	12,458	12,514	56
2/26/04	Sandy Betts	12,704*	12,768	64
2/26/04	Networking meeting	12,768*	12,790	22

* Odometer readings are not necessarily in order, because this car is being used for personal travel as well as business.

expenses and depreciation. Again, it pays to calculate both ways and see which works out to your benefit.

All your vehicle expenses can be tracked in many ways—but as always, the simpler the better. Save each receipt, write on it whether it was incurred for business or not, and put it with your business receipts. I have found that charging all my gas on one particular card makes it easier for me to calculate the total. (You'll still need to retain the receipts, though.)

Recording mileage is a bit more tedious. If you are using your car for both personal and business reasons, you'll need to create a system that works for you. I confess, I haven't been very good at this, but I'm getting better. I tried recording my totals in a mileage log like the one above, noting the odometer reading when I started and ended each trip, but that didn't seem to work for me. I found it much easier to track the number of miles to a client's home or business appointment, then write this down next to the entry for that appointment in my calendar. At the end of the year, I go through my calendar and add up all the mileage. Whatever method you choose, though, be consistent and scrupulous about capturing all your business miles. (See blank milage record on page 215 to get you started.)

Filing the Return

Most home-based professional organizing businesses are either sole proprietorships or LLCs. Because these business types are not incorporated, the earnings and deductions are passed through to you and must be reported on your individual taxes, Form 1040. Sole proprietors use Schedule C to report the profit and loss; LLCs use Schedule E.

There is an additional step for LLCs, however. Just as an individual submits a return to the IRS, so must the business entity or LLC. Form 1065 is used for this purpose, with the necessary information being given to the partners on a K1. The K1 in turn provides you with the information to include on Schedule E. Since you report your profit or loss from your business on your personal taxes, you must have your business taxes completed first and in time to include on your personal taxes.

To have an accountant prepare your tax returns for your business can cost anywhere from $350 to $2,000, depending on your business entity, size, and activity. The software out there for tax preparation, like Quicken and TurboTax, costs anywhere from $60 to $200.

Helpful IRS Publications

- Publication 334, *Tax Guide for Small Business*
- Publication 505, *Tax Withholding and Estimated Tax*
- Publication 533, *Self-Employment Tax*
- Publication 534, *Depreciation*
- Publication 535, *Business Expenses*
- Publication 541, *Tax Information on Partnerships*
- Publication 583, *Starting a Business and Keeping Records*
- Publication 587, *Business Use of Your Home*
- Publication 917, *Business Use of Your Car*

04

Training, Tools, and Tips for the Professional

Odds are that you already know the basics of what it takes to be a professional organizer. Even so, if you've never organized for anyone other than friends and family, the different expectations a paying client will have of you—and the difference in your own expectations of yourself—can come as a bit of a shock. This chapter will help you through this transition by preparing you to handle all types of situations in a professional manner.

Training and Education

You may have strong skills when it comes to organizing, but before you start working with clients, it may be beneficial to get some coaching, training, or even apprenticing under your belt.

Although no specific training or certification is required to become a professional organizer, formalized training offers lots of benefits. There are many opportunities for this training, and it's up to you to determine which method works best for you. You surely already bring a particular skill set with you to the organizing business—talents that you have developed in a previous work situation, or skills that you've perfected working at home or with friends and family. Work now to create situations in which you can polish and refine these skills, and then take advantage of them when you start your business.

Apprenticeships

Learning from a seasoned organizer will always be a valuable experience. Sure, you may already be aware of how to clean a closet or organize a garage, but working with someone who has been in the business for a while can provide knowledge that will save you time, money, and probably lots of headaches. Some organizing companies offer courses or apprenticeships in professional organizing. I have trained many new organizers, and some have chosen to apprentice with me. Once your training is complete, you'll have a ready-made roster of clients, not to mention the opportunity to either work side by side with another organizer or receive immediate feedback on your work. All of this will go a long way toward refining your skills and building your career. If you can find such a situation, consider this a sound business investment and take advantage of it!

Mentoring or Coaching

Mentoring or coaching can be particularly helpful to new organizers who may already have clients, but still lack confidence. Even if you don't live nearby, a mentor or coach can provide you with invaluable training. I once coached a new organizer halfway across the country. She had lived in my area, taken my training course, and apprenticed with me. Then she moved back to her home state several thousand miles away. Since she still wasn't sure she was ready to venture out on her own, we designed a program that allowed her to continue "practicing" her organizing skills under the watchful eye of someone who had been in the business for quite a while. I spoke over the phone with her while viewing pictures and videos of clients' homes; we did this weekly with each client until she felt comfortable venturing out on her own.

Industry Workshops

Associations and organizations provide workshops and seminars that support professional organizers. These workshops are often taught at yearly meetings; some associations meet on a local level and offer workshops routinely throughout the year. Find out if there is a chapter near you and see what it has to offer.

On-the-Job Training

There is also the old-fashioned way of learning: on the job. (I don't recommend this to someone who has never organized before.) If this is the route you plan to take, then I suggest you become familiar with appendix B, "Recommended Reading." You'll want to educate yourself in many areas of organizing and be prepared to do some studying between client visits. The real trick here is always to keep a step or two ahead of your clients. If you anticipate a need for a particular organizing system, you have time between visits to do the research and bring in the information or skills necessary to complete the task. Sometimes we learn best when we challenge ourselves.

Certification

As I've mentioned, there is no requirement to be certified. However, NAPO (National Association of Professional Organizers) has a voluntary, industry lead certification process that recognizes, through examination and client interactions, professional organizers as CPO's—Certified Professional Organizers. Also, if you're interested in working with the chronically disorganized, the NSGCD (National Study Group for the Chronically Disorganized) has their own specific training program and examination that certifies you based on their particular requirements and standards of working with the this population.. I'm proud to say that the book you are reading is on the list of recommended reading for the NAPO CPO examination

I'm Not an Organizer, But I Play One on TV

I know you've seen those celebrity designers on television come up with home-decorating plans and organizational systems on the fly—most of the time without the homeowners' involvement. But remember, this is TV! It's entertainment first, information second. You never see the after-effects, once clients move back in and struggle to work in a system that was designed without their input. While some things might stick, I can tell you that a system designed without client input can be disastrous. Besides, if you look closely enough at the final results you see on TV, a true organizer can poke holes in many of the systems these designers set up. Much of the work you see on these shows is done purely for flash and effect!

I think of training as akin to playing the piano. You may indeed know how to play a song or two, but if you take lessons, your playing gets stronger and better.

4 Steps to Organizing Anything

Friends or family typically won't demand that you finish a project within a certain amount of time, but you can bet that a paying client will. That means you have to have a plan for how you will proceed with each step of your project—on time and on budget. You also have to be prepared for the unknown. Toward that end, I'm going to share with you the 4 Steps to Organizing Anything, a process I have long recommended to beginning organizers. With this 4-Step formula in your bag, so to speak, you will be ready for any organizing situation. If you ever feel like you're getting snowed under, these principles can provide you with a sort of road map through the storm.

When I first decided to become an organizer, I read every book with the word *organize* in it that I could get my hands on. I found great tips and techniques for organizing all areas of the home and office. There are whole books dedicated solely to dealing with paperwork! I read, and read, and kept filling up my brain with all the many ways to organize, use a container, find a product, and more. But when it came time to working with clients, I realized that I needed a method to systematically evaluate and plan the work we were about to do, to ensure that the organizational systems that we designed would meet their needs. It wasn't enough to know what containers would work or even to know what other organizers had done for their clients. It would be critical for me to design filing and organizational systems specifically geared to how my clients lived and moved in their space.

Clients are anxious creatures. Most ask a thousand questions. And in the beginning I thought I had to have all the answers. So I'd try to put together an elaborate plan describing down to the last detail how the room would look and what systems we would put into place. What I realized through trial and error is that trying to figure out the end result of our project before we even started was pure craziness. It's like a doctor giving someone a treatment before diagnosing the problem. I would have a whole design as to how the room would look and how we were going to set it up and what supplies we would use, and halfway through I'd notice that it wasn't making sense anymore. There's just no way for organizers to know what someone needs until they start digging into the mess.

Once I realized that I didn't have to have all the answers right away, it was easy to stop a client's barrage of questions with a simple "I'm not sure yet; we don't have enough information." The client would relax, and we could proceed. I realized that all I needed to do was keep one or two steps ahead of my client—not a hundred miles.

To stay the proverbial two steps ahead, I realized I needed a flexible but dependable process to guide me as I navigated the unpredictable waters I was traveling with my clients. I thought back to my nursing days and pulled out an old care plan. This was a document we medical professionals used to help us plan patients' care in a way that ensured we covered everything but also tailored our efforts to their specific needs. Although I dreaded using this process when I was a student nurse, because it seemed so tedious, I realize now there was a reason I learned these 4 Steps. I could have never imagined then that this 4-Step formula would come in handy so many years later, and for such a different purpose.

The **4 Steps** are:

1. Assess
2. Plan
3. Implement
4. Evaluate

Using these steps provides you with a methodical, systematic way to work your way through even the most overwhelming of messes. It can be applied to the trunk of car, a kitchen, a garage—virtually anywhere you intend to organize. These 4 Steps have proven to be the backbone of the work I do with clients. Use this process as a sound basis for your practice, learning and growing and getting creative from there!

I will explain each step in detail. If you can work according to these principles, you'll be well on your way to custom-designing solutions that will satisfy the individual needs of each of your clients.

Step 1: Assess

This first step, in my opinion, is the most critical. It helps you understand how the client thinks and gives you clues as to how to proceed. In the next chapter I'll tell you more about how using this step factors into the initial client visit. For now we'll focus on its general purpose.

Each new project begins with an assessment visit, during which you get an overview of your client's entire situation. As you begin to work with the client, you will use this assessment phase again every time you turn to a new specific project or area.

Remember, it's not our job as professional organizers to be mind readers. The more questions we ask, the more information we have to design the perfect system.

Here are the main questions you need to answer during the assessment phase:

- What's working?
- What's not working?
- What are the essential items needed for this space?
- What's causing the M.E.S.S.?

What's Working?

During your first visit and then again whenever you start a new project, you will ask clients what they think works well in their space and what they especially like about it. Typically they'll instead launch into a list of their complaints, what they don't like, or what's not working; your job is to steer them back to thinking about what they *do* like. There's always something that's working in every space. Help them find what it is. This information is key to seeing how they operate and figuring out what their style might be. Once you've heard them out, ask them to finish these sentences:

- I can always find . . .
- I like the fact that . . .
- I like using . . .
- This space works because . . .

Look for clues to help you ask the right questions. Let's say you notice a belt rack in the midst of a chaotic walk-in closet. It's perfectly hung, with a belt on each peg. You say to your clients, "Tell me about the belt rack." They go on to tell you a story about a beautiful wooden belt rack, made of teak, from the island of wherever, that they got on their honeymoon...and so on and so on. If this happens, you can assume

Don't Assume

When working with a client, it's hard not to get caught up in trying to figure things out too quickly, or assume you can jump to the answers before the client even says anything. My suggestion to you is to listen...really listen to what the client says at these critical stages. I had a client not too long ago that had a path from the door to the two chairs in the living room. Each room in the home was completely saturated with stuff. One could assume, as I began to, that the client had a hoarding and/or shopping problem. Ten minutes into the assessment she tells me her husband had recently died—as in seven days prior. She told me none of this was her stuff and that she only lived like this to accommodate her dying husband. I had suspicions still. However, within several months time we had dug out from under it all, and her place was showroom perfect. And I'm proud to say that she has maintained it to this day.

that your clients are driven by a desire for aesthetics as well as function and have emotional connections to seemingly innocuous objects. If you replace their jumble of leftover dry-cleaner hangers with all-wooden hangers, it may inspire them to maintain their space. So continue to help them notice what else is working: "I like shelves instead of drawers"; "I prefer hanging to folding"; "I'm a minimalist." All this information is key to designing a system that complements your clients' style.

It's also important to identify what works because, as they say, "If it ain't broke, don't fix it!" Once you've identified what works, you'll want to model other systems on it. Think of it this way: If you take the room apart, when you put it back together again, be sure you put back the parts that worked.

What's Not Working?

Next, ask clients to tell you what they don't like about the space—what they believe doesn't work for them. This is usually an easier question for them to answer—it's probably why they called you in the first place! Let them get it all out while you listen very closely to what they are saying. Listen even to what they're not saying.

While standing in the space with clients, have them finish these phrases:

- I can never find . . .
- I'm tired of . . .
- I have no place for . . .
- I don't like this space because . . .

The answers to these questions will give you a good idea of what problems you need to create solutions for. If one of the complaints is that your client's husband reads the newspaper every evening and leaves it all over the living room—well, there's not much you can do about the husband. But creating a place where the newspaper can be stored close to the husband's favorite chair, instead of the recycle bin in the back hall, may go a long way toward eliminating the problem. Focus on the problems you can solve, not the personal ones the client inadvertently advertises.

I had a client who, during our tour through her bedroom, began complaining about her dresser. The drawers wouldn't pull out correctly; they were too shallow; she didn't even like how the handles felt in her hand. Then she grumbled about the side table and the bed itself. I had to pose the question that seemed to be begging to be asked: "Tell me about this bedroom set?" She paused for a moment, then said, "It was my husband's from his first marriage." Well, that's all I needed to hear. I told her that all the organizing in the world couldn't fix that problem. We talked about some possible solutions and finally decided to move the furniture to their guest room and begin searching for the perfect bedroom set for her and her husband.

Essential Items

What are the essential items needed to make this space user friendly, manageable, and attractive? What are the events, tasks, and activities that go on here, and what is required for these activities? Knowing the answers to these questions is very important because it will allow you the freedom to move items out of the area and create more space for what really belongs there.

I had a client tell me she was tired of having her three children's books and papers all over the kitchen table—but she went on to tell me that this was where they did their homework. The solution was simple: While storage for books and backpacks isn't essential in most kitchens, for this client it was. My client had three ample cabinets in which she stored party and off-season items. These were easy to relocate to the pantry; the cabinets and the drawers above them could then be allotted for school items. Now each child had a storage area for essential items! This solution immediately eliminated the after-homework battle of getting the table cleared for dinner. It also was great in the morning, when the kids could just grab their backpacks for the postbreakfast dash to the bus. The client had never thought to make storage room for these items, but once they were identified as essential, we made the change—and instantly the clutter was eliminated. The client was thrilled.

What's Causing the M.E.S.S.?

Is it a **M**echanical, **E**motional, **S**ituational, or **S**ystem problem?

Mechanical

The pantry door is off its track, the drawer is broken, and the handle fell off two years ago: These types of mechanical problems can be fixed, usually with a quick twist of a screwdriver or tap of a hammer. Sometimes the problem has gone on for so long, the client doesn't even notice it anymore. Some mechanical problems take a bit more elbow grease to rectify, but identifying them is always your first step.

During each assessment I carry around a great product—a stick lubricant with silicone (more on my favorite products later). Whenever I spot a drawer that's stuck or a door that seems to be too hard to open, I ask clients first if I can use the product, then apply the lubricant...and years of sticky-drawer syndrome melt away. Clients are thrilled, and I have just turned into a magician. They are encouraged and excited to know that some solutions may be just that simple.

Emotional

Aunt Sally gave it to me. I've had this since college. Danny made that for me when he was in first grade. I bought that on our honeymoon. I can't get rid of this, I spent good money on it! You name it, you'll hear it when it comes to the emotional attachments people have to their stuff. Hopefully by the time they've called you, they've reached the point where they're ready to let go and the emotional attachments will be more easily broken. If not, you have your work cut out for you.

One quick fix is to simply make sure that these items are being identified and stored appropriately. For instance, that T-shirt from college—which they will never wear again but cannot seem to part with—should be with other keepsake items, maybe in a box or trunk, but not the dresser drawer. Some clients don't realize the reason they are holding on to something is emotional until you say, "Tell me about this?" and they go on to tell you that they'd never use it but "It reminds me of . . ." This is your first clue!

I once had a client who owned many, many trophies. Every time he read the name plates—MVP 1978; BEST BOWLER 1988; TOP SALES 1996; EMPLOYEE OF THE YEAR—he'd grow nostalgic and insist he could never part with them. I suggested he remove the name plates from the trophies, put them on a single board, and frame it. He loved the idea. Out went more than thirty trophies, replaced by one framed piece on the wall.

Situational

Have your clients recently moved, gotten a divorce, had a baby, or relocated their offices? In other words, has some recent event created a major interruption in their life or space? If so, you need to recognize that your clients' issues are situational and you must work with them in setting up temporary systems to get them through this transition. Later on, they'll be more settled and have more information as to their needs.

When clients are dealing with major life changes, it's often difficult to clearly envision all the organizational systems they will need. I certainly recommend that they get started, but remember as you set up systems that it may take a bit longer than usual to determine whether these systems are working. Allowing and encouraging clients to function in their space for a while will give them a chance to discover what they like and don't like, need and don't need, about the space or setup. So often I've seen clients make purchases too early during a transitional time, only to have them not work properly. And when a system isn't working properly, you get clutter.

System

Is it the system itself that isn't working? Many people set up systems that are too cumbersome. Remember that simple is better. Look at the systems clients have in place: Can the number of steps be cut down? Are there ways to make the system easier? Let's say your client complains that her foyer closet is always a wreck, particularly in winter when her child's coat is forever on the floor. You take a look at the closet and realize that to hang up his coat properly, the child would have to open the closet door, pull up a step stool, stretch to grab a hanger, hang his coat, put away the stool, and then shut the door. Well, no wonder his coat is on the floor! The solution, of course, is to let the child hang his coat on an easy-access peg. You see my point.

Before and After

Everyone loves to look at before-and-after pictures of organizing projects. I always try to be respectful of my clients' discomfort and possible embarrassment over their current clutter situation, however, and never ask to take pictures during the assessment visit. I do often suggest that clients take pictures prior to our first work session, or I offer to take pictures at our first work session if they don't have a camera handy. I tell them that at this point, I'll use the photos only as a record of our progress. When we finish with the job and I take the after pictures, though, I usually find that clients are so proud of them, they're happy to let me share them with others in printed materials or on my website. I have them sign a release form prior to using any pictures (see Photo Consent Form on page 216).

Assessment takes place during your first visit, but it doesn't stop there. You will continue to gather information as you move through the organizing process with your clients, especially each time you turn to a new project or area.

Step 2: Plan

To create a plan you must sit down with clients and determine what exactly will make them satisfied with their space. I don't mean that they need to come up with how it will be organized or even how it will look—that's what they're paying you for. Still, you do need to extract from them their expectations for the space. What would make them happy? They might say, "I would love it if I could find my stamps when I need them," or "It would be nice if I had a place to fold laundry when it came out of the dryer." This is the point where clients get to identify and share with you their dreams for the space.

Until now all they thought they wanted was less mess and clutter. Your job is to help them see beyond that. You want them to see the possibilities for the ultimate in workstations or the best pantry on the block. They may have a hard time describing their vision right now, but keep asking the questions. As the process unfolds, clients will get better at telling you what they want. The more they can verbalize what will make them happy with their space, the more you know about how to help them achieve it. Along the way, of course, you'll become the organizer they talk about to everyone they know.

Another part of the planning phase is calculating how long will it take to finish the job. There are, unfortunately, no hard-and-fast rules for determining project timetables, but it may help you to remember that the key components are your clients' ability to make decisions and the volume of stuff you're working with. The assessment phase gave you a chance to size up clients' working style—are they quick to make decisions or slow to process their thoughts? Take this information

Some Helpful Time Estimates

Here's how long it takes, on the average, to organize:

- A closet: 4–8 hours

- A bedroom: 8–12 hours

- A kitchen: 10–14 hours

- A garage: 8–12 hours

- An office (including the filing system): 16–24 hours

into account as you make your time estimates. The better you get at sizing up your clients and identifying the extent of their possessions—and any hidden adventures these may contain—the closer to reality your time estimates will be.

Step 3: Implement

This is the step where you and the client dig in. You are about to implement a new L.E.A.S.E. on life. That's the acronym I use to describe the various components of this step.

L = Like with Like

No surprise here: Implementing starts when you take a look at the cabinet, drawer, closet, desktop—whatever space you're working on—then pull out each item, one after the other, and place it with like items. For instance, all the pants go in one pile, all the sweaters go together, all the pencils get their own stack, and so on. Start at one end and keep going until the whole space is empty. Remind your clients that this is a quick sort—no decisions need to be made here. They come in the next step.

Clients do have their own categories for things—they may just not know it yet. For instance, I had a client who wore certain clothes only on her summer vacation. Each time we came across such a piece, we put it into a "vacation clothes" pile. The client liked this category, because it made perfect sense to her. When we were finished she said, "I don't need to keep these in my closet; let's put them right in a suitcase and I'll store them elsewhere." It was a great solution that meant no more searching for her favorite vacation outfits, *and* more space in her closet. The moral? Don't limit yourself to the obvious categories, like "summer clothes" or "winter clothes." Here are some examples of like-with-like categories:

- Work clothes
- Play clothes
- Guest towels
- Travel supplies
- Baking supplies
- And so on, and so on!

Remember that old college T-shirt? This is the moment when you want to identify it as a keepsake and start a pile for keepsakes. Most clients have more keepsakes—objects that aren't useful or practical but are kept for sentimental

A Word from the Wise(r)

Early in my career I worked with a client reorganizing her kitchen. I was so excited to get my career off the ground that before I knew it, my client and I had each and every cabinet emptied and were filling up every horizontal surface available, including three folding tables she brought in from the garage. Then I looked down at my watch and realized that in forty-five minutes, her children would be home from school. I had to get her kitchen in working order before then! Panic overwhelmed me. How in the world could we get this kitchen reassembled?

Well, we couldn't. Our session ran about an hour past schedule and we had to box up one section of her kitchen in temporary storage. The client was okay with this—she didn't realize that this wasn't how professional organizers were suppose to work! I knew otherwise, unfortunately. I'd have to do a much better job next time at some crucial tasks. One was keeping an eye on the clock. Another was tackling one part of the project at a time, instead of trying to do it all in one session; for a kitchen, that might mean working on food items one day, for instance, and dishes another. And I needed to block out longer working sessions for larger projects. Sometimes there's nothing like on-the-job training to really send a point home.

reasons—than they realize. There's another category that might come in handy here, too: home decorating. Why not? You could suggest the client frame the T-shirt and hang it on a family room wall. Same thing for old record albums. If your clients are unlikely to actually listen to them anymore, they make decorative additions to a rec room or study!

E = Eliminate

Now it's time to take a closer look at each pile, eliminating the unused, broken, ugly, unnecessary, and old. It can be donated, returned, trashed—doesn't matter; if your clients aren't using it, it doesn't belong there. This process of elimination is easier, of course, once all like items are together. It may be hard for someone to part with a black sweater until she sees all eight of her black sweaters together in a pile. Then she'll begin to realize this one is scratchy, that one doesn't fit right, this one is outdated, but this one she loves! That's why eliminating is a no-no during the like-with-like step. Wait until you've sorted everything with clients. Only then will they get on board.

Have boxes labeled and ready to go for donations, trash, or items being moved elsewhere in the house. That ELSEWHERE IN THE HOUSE box is especially important, because you don't want clients running around trying to put things away. Just place the items in this box; you'll deal with them later.

At the end of the elimination phase, there is typically a whole lot less stuff to put back into the space you are organizing.

A = Assign a Home

You have now worked through all the objects or papers in your target space. Ignoring anything you've deemed trash or charity, approach each remaining object with the questions, *Is this your rightful place? Is this where you truly belong?* Remember that old saying, "Everything has a place?" Referring back to the list of essential items that you identified in the assessment step, and then to your plan, determine where every item belongs.

Next, look for a place where all like items can be stored together. The pants should hang together in one spot in the closet, not some down here, others over there. Same thing goes for other like items: All the batteries should be in one place, all the wrapping supplies, all the holiday decorations.

S = Shop

You've conducted triage on your clients' possessions, and you've decided where must-keep items should live. Now you're ready to come up with storage ideas. You're heading into what for many of us organizers is the most enjoyable step of all...shopping!

You can shop the Internet or catalogs, but the best place to start is in your clients' homes, using the containers they already own (often things they've purchased in previous attempts to get organized). These are temporary solutions designed to give you some feedback on the solutions you're proposing.

Let's say you think setting up a basket to collect all the shoes at the door is a good idea, but you have no basket right now. Well, just set up a cardboard box until your next visit. This will give you a chance to see if your suggestion works for your clients, as well as helping you calculate what size basket they will need. You can use old shoe boxes to mimic drawer dividers and office storage containers. I once used two very long ice coolers under about five file crates to mimic the look of a credenza for the client. She actually used it for about three weeks and loved how it was working for her; in the meantime we searched for the perfect style credenza to fit her office.

Another client had massive amounts of paper to review on a daily basis. As a fund manager, he received anywhere from 8 to 20 inches' worth of paper weekly for each fund—and he was in charge of about fifteen funds! As you can imagine, his desk was completely consumed by paper. His routine was to pick out a stack of papers, go into the living room, review the information...then leave all the nonessential paper behind on the living room floor.

The solution? Decorative garbage bins, 10 by 14 inches and about a foot and a half high. We purchased fifteen nice-looking square wooden garbage bins and placed them on top of a large credenza behind his desk. Each bin was labeled with the fund it represented. All papers from that fund were stacked in the bin. My client could review the fund there in his office or carry the bin and papers to wherever he chose. He also devised a system whereby he used a colored piece of paper to separate the papers he didn't want to keep from those he had reviewed and wanted to save. When a bin got full, he removed the discarded papers and kept the system going.

Voilà: My client had a clear desk, and his family had a clean living room. This solution changed their lives instantly!

E = Equalize

Equalizing means maintaining a clean and balanced space on a daily basis, and it's the responsibility of your clients. I tell my own clients that it should take no longer than five minutes per room to get everything back to its place. Equalizing a desktop—which shouldn't take more than ten minutes—involves reviewing daily work, identifying priorities for the following day, and leaving the space clean and organized.

If these processes take longer than five or ten minutes, then one of your systems needs evaluation. That's the fourth and final step in the organizing process.

Store It Where You Use It

As my client and I cleaned out a linen closet in her hallway, she identified nail polish as an essential item. She'd always stored her nail polish here, near her makeup and other beauty products, and this is where she wanted it.

When we got to the assign-a-home stage, though, she started to reconsider. She realized she invariably applied nail polish at the kitchen table. This meant that she was forever climbing the stairs to the linen closet to get the polish, and often leaving it on the stairs to take down with her to the table. Based on my store-it-where-you-use-it rule, it dawned on her that her nail polish, remover, and some cotton balls should be housed in a kitchen cabinet. We collected all these items, placed them in a small container, and relocated them to the kitchen. No more piles of nail supplies on the steps!

Step 4: Evaluate

Are the organizational or filing systems you have created functioning well? Are they easy for your clients to use? Do clients feel their lives have gotten easier? As you progress through organizing projects with clients, it's critical that you evaluate past projects on a continuing basis. Talk to your clients: What's working? What isn't? What adjustments need to be made?

Respond to all this feedback immediately, tweaking and fine-tuning your work whether that means making changes in object placement, in your choice of products, or in the process itself. Allow a little time to pass to see how those adjustments are working. Hopefully your clients have been learning some of your techniques throughout the organizing sessions, too, and will be able to make adjustments as needed after you're gone.

This is also the point where you might want to send out postcard reminders of "Spring Cleaning" or "Seasonal Spruce-Up." Once clients know how good it feels to be organized, they often want you to come in and give then a hand occasionally as their lives grow and change! And the beat goes on . . .

●　　●　　●

Assess. Plan. Implement. Evaluate. These are the four steps to organizing anything. If you use this process, I guarantee that you will never feel overwhelmed by even the biggest chaos.

Paperwork Power

Paperwork has been the biggest surprise for me as an organizer. It has been involved in almost every organizing project I have worked on. Even if you don't identify paperwork as a target problem during the assessment phase, you'll soon find that most clients are in need of a good filing system. I've discovered while working in clients' bedrooms that they store their important papers such as birth certificates and property deeds in their jewelry boxes. Others might have a filing cabinet with twenty-year-old documents mixed in with current yoga schedules and insurance papers. I've even encountered folks who've devoted entire rooms to excess paper. They routinely shove all the papers they don't know what to do with into bags, and into the room they go. I guess you can call that a file room!

Fortunately, dealing with paper can be one of the most rewarding parts of this job. I have found that creating filing systems for individuals and small-business owners makes an almost magical difference in their lives. It does take time, especially in the beginning—an hour or more for each foot-high stack of paper. But as you progress it gets easier and easier.

In chapter 2 we discussed setting up your personal office filing system. If you haven't gotten your own files in order, now is the time! I've worked with many organizing students who thought they had a good system for maintaining their own paperwork, only to convert their systems over to the new way I taught them when they realized how much more efficient it is. Also, your own filing system is a great place to try out the following tips and techniques. I developed my home filing system when I decided it was time to combine my husband's papers with my own. We had been married for about five years at the time, and it was a great opportunity to combine some of our stuff. Indeed, this system works great to this day. We both can find and put back the files we need easily, and we add new files and remove old ones with ease.

Paper filing and retrieval should be simple. Clients should be able to retrieve any paper in less than a minute. That said, some clients are convinced that they have a good system for their paperwork...they just can't figure out why there are still papers all over their counters, dining room tables, and desktops. The answer is that they *don't* have a good filing system. If they did, it would be working for them!

The most critical tip I can give you is this: Filing cabinets or portable file containers should be located within reach of where the paper is being dealt with. In an office, for instance, files should be within arm's length of the desk. If the file cabinet is close but not reachable, the filing will not get done. At home, it's not good enough to have an office upstairs or down in the basement if paperwork is being dealt with in the kitchen or living room. The piles will continue until your clients have a system that lets them file and retrieve within arm's reach of where they do the paperwork.

Let's go through a typical paper sort with a client.

Paper Sort Supplies
- Manila file folders
- Trash can/recycle bin
- "How Long Do I Keep It" list
- Pencils
- The clients' to-do list
- Post-its
- Drinks
- Music

Start wherever you've decided to locate the client's information center. Visible papers come first—these are usually the most active. If your clients have not looked at a particular file in a year or more, put it in a box, label it, and set it aside for later.

There are two questions to ask about each piece of paper: "What is this?" and "Why are you saving it?" Let's say you find a flyer that lists local real estate agents along with their recently sold properties. Are your clients saving this because they're thinking of listing their house? Or are they Realtors themselves and keeping the flyer because they like its design? Whatever the case, knowing why a piece of paper is there is critical to filing it properly.

Now put the paper in a manila file folder and give it a name—in pencil. Choose the name with retrieval in mind, not storage, meaning you want to use whatever words would come most readily to your clients' minds when they want to find the file. If they're saving veterinary records for their dog Max, for instance, they might name the file VET VISITS, DOG STUFF, or MAX. The real estate flyer could be filed under HOUSE SALE PREP or MARKETING IDEAS. A vehicle file could be labeled CAR, TRUCK, or AUTO...or maybe VAN or WAGON, or even VOLVO or HONDA. The names you choose should reflect what clients will be thinking when they go to look for the file.

The Name Game

I have a client I've been working with sporadically for years. We established a filing system the first year we worked together, and she has maintained it well over the years. At a recent visit she admitted to never really understanding the term "Vital Records" and admitted to looking in several drawers before finding where the file was. Even though the file was a specific color, it was the name that was throwing her off. I suggested renaming this category of personal family information papers. This file represents specifics to her and her family, such as birth certificates, resumes, insurance papers, health records—all of their personal or vital statistics. She came up with "Documents" simple but clear and she knows them as the blue ones. I don't care what the category is called and neither should you. If it works for the client, that's the part that counts. She said with that one little change it made it easier for her retrieve the file she was looking for.

I also recommend using words that enable clients to keep like files together in the system: for example, CAR—BMW and CAR—Volkswagen. If the word CAR precedes the term clients prefer, then all the files will be alphabetized together in the drawer.

As in any other organizing project, once folders start accumulating you want to group like with like. With files, it's harder to see the categories until you've created twenty or thirty and begin sorting. Take a look at the sample categories I've offered for you on page 84 to get clients started with the concept. Once they realize that their files will be broken up into these categories, they begin to get it and can easily tell you which categories they think their files belong in. This process can be very liberating for clients; they begin to see some light at the end of their very long paperwork tunnel. All their financial papers are together, all their vital records are together, and all their schedules and other everyday papers are together as well.

Once you've grouped them together, decide on a color for each category. Place colored dots on each file folder to designate which category they are in. Put each category in its own container. For instance, you might put a green dot on all the financial files and place them in a drawer or file box together.

Avoid creating file names such as URGENT, MISC., or PENDING. If some papers are transient—they will be dealt with and then tossed—they can go into a WORKING file. This file would include such items as invitations, surveys, and envelopes with return addresses on them. Clients will RSVP to the invite, record it in their calendar, and toss the invite. They complete the survey then mail it off. The new address of an old friend will be recorded in an address book and the envelope tossed.

Don't read any papers or take action during a paper sort. Stopping to peruse that interesting article torn out of a magazine, or that recipe, or those letters, or that appraisal done on the house doesn't just slow down the process, it brings it to a grinding halt. Remember, this is a *quick* sort. File everything even if it needs action. Have clients create a to-do list to remind themselves of important tasks. If you stop to read or take action right now, there would be no time for organizing!

Allow clients to work with their file folders for a week or two—longer if need be. They may need to move a file from one category to another, depending on their preference. For instance, they may have at first put their RECEIPTS file in the Vital Records category, but decide that it actually belongs in the Financial category. They might also realize that some files or categories need new names.

The next step is getting the files into their colored, labeled folders. I recommend Smead two-ply colored 1/3-cut files. You've spent time creating this system, and you want quality folders that won't get dog-eared as they are being used.

Last of all comes permanent labeling of the files. I use a Casio label maker always with black ink on white tape and all-capital letters for easy reading.

Additional Filing Tips

- Make a list of the new files to leave with your clients until they get used to them.
- Use straight tab filing—that is, with all tabs either left, right, or center, not alternating. Straight tab filing is much easier on the eye, and files can be added or deleted anytime without ruining the pattern.
- Use alphabetical (A–Z) order within each category.
- Store regularly used files where they're used; the remaining files in that category can be located in another area. For instance, if your clients do most of their paperwork in the kitchen, pull the most used files from each category and store them in a portable file box on the kitchen counter. If clients are dealing with a medical issue right now, be sure those files are close by—but there's no reason for (say) life insurance papers to take up space in the active file box. These can be kept in the Vital Records drawer, back in the office.
- To stop incoming junk mail, call (888) 567-8688 or visit www.optoutprescreen.com.
- If your clients already have a filing system, but it isn't working for them, start over from scratch and then incorporate their old files into your new system. Trying to fix an old system is sometimes more trouble than it's worth. The products that you recommend will also most likely be better than what they're currently using.

How Long Should I Keep It?

Clients are forever asking me this question. My suggestion is that you provide them with the following list, making adjustments based on their preferences.

When my husband and I first sat down to sort through our paperwork together, he was amazed at how much I had. After we started going through them, I realized

Pencil Me In

Always label your temporary file folders in pencil. Why? For one thing, this allows you to reuse the files later on by simply erasing the name. Also, this makes it easy to change the file's name if your clients tell you, "I think I like AUTO instead of CAR."

I didn't need my cable TV bills from the past four years. They're not tax deductible, I'd certainly never reviewed them—and if I wanted to, the cable company has them on record. So what was I keeping them for? I tossed them that very day and never looked back. One less piece of paper to file! Remind your clients to check with their accountant, tax adviser, or spouse prior to getting rid of any papers in question. This is doubly true for anyone who runs any type of business from the home.

How Long Should You Keep It?

- **Auto records:** As long as you own the vehicle.
- **Appointment books (past):** Up to ten years, depending on your comfort level.
- **ATM slips:** Until reconciled, store these with your bank statement.
- **Credit card statements:** Six years for tax-related purchases; otherwise, until you receive the interest statement issued by the company annually.
- **Catalogs and magazines:** Until the next issue arrives.
- **Dividend payment records:** Until you receive your annual statement.
- **Health records:** Permanently.
- **Home improvements:** As long as you own the home. Store these with your tax records.
- **Household inventory and appraisal:** As long as they're current. Update these annually.
- **Insurance policies** (auto, homeowners, liability): Through the statute of limitations.
- **Insurance policies** (disability, medical, life, personal property, umbrella): For the life of the policy.
- **Investment purchase records:** As long as you own the investments.
- **Investment sales records:** Six years for tax purposes.

- **Mortgage or loan discharge:** As long as you own the home, or six years after the discharge.
- **Pay stubs:** Until they're verified by a W-2 statement.
- **Property bill of purchase:** As long as you own the property.
- **Receipts:** As long as they're current, or as determined by your accountant.
- **Résumés:** Until they're superseded.
- **Safe-deposit box key and inventory:** As long as they're current.
- **Tax records:** Current year plus six years prior (check with your accountant).
- **Utility bills:** Until they're paid (unless you're planning to deduct them for home office use).
- **Vital records and documents** (such as birth certificates and medical records): Permanently.
- **Wills, trusts, estate plans:** Permanently.

Safe-Deposit Box Items

- Adoption papers
- Automobile title
- Birth certificates
- Citizenship papers
- Copyrights or patents
- Death certificates
- Divorce decrees
- Life insurance policies
- Marriage certificates
- Military discharge papers
- Passports
- Property deeds
- Powers of attorney
- Wills, trusts, and estate plan

Some Sample File Categories

Financial

- 401(K)
- BANK STATEMENTS
- CLOSED ACCOUNTS
- CREDIT CARD AGREEMENTS
- HEALTH CARE EXPENSES
- MORTGAGES
- MUTUAL FUND
- PAY STUBS
- PENSION
- PHONE BILLS
- RECEIPTS
- STOCKS
- STUDENT LOAN
- UTILITIES

Lifestyle

- DOG TRAINING
- FAMILY HISTORY
- HEALTH/VITAMINS/DIET
- HUMOR
- KEEPSAKES—DAD
- KEEPSAKES—KARLI
- KEEPSAKES—MOM
- LANDSCAPE IDEAS
- MAPS
- MENUS
- SCRABBLE CLUB
- SHORE TRIP
- TRAIN/BUS SCHEDULES
- TRAVEL
- VACATION IDEAS
- WARRANTIES/INSTRUCTIONS
- WISH LIST

Vital Records

- ADVANCE DIRECTIVES
- CAR INSURANCE
- CAR LOANS/TITLE
- CAR REPAIRS
- CERTIFICATES—BIRTH/MARRIAGE
- CREDIT REPORT
- EZ PASS
- FREQUENT FLIER
- HEALTH RECORDS—DAD
- HEALTH RECORDS—KARLI
- HEALTH RECORDS—MOM
- INSURANCE—HEALTH
- INSURANCE—HOMEOWNERS
- RÉSUMÉ—MOM
- SOCIAL SECURITY STATEMENTS
- TITLE INSURANCE

Working Files/Desktop

- AWAITING CALLBACK/DELIVERY TO COME
- CALLS TO MAKE
- INFO TO CAPTURE (a temporary holding spot for things like business cards or scraps of paper with phone numbers and addresses, movies to see, books to read, etc., that haven't been put in their more permanent retrieval location yet)
- RSVPS
- TO DO
- TO FILE

Your Workbag

Over my years as a professional organizer, I've put together a list of basic supplies that I keep with me at all times. I feel like a modern-day Mary Poppins when I reach into my workbag, often pulling out a simple item that seems to work magic on my clients' space—they're awed. I love my bag. Even when I'm not working with clients, I carry it in the car with me. You never know when you'll run into an organizing emergency!

My main workbag contains the following essentials. Of course, if I am working on special projects with clients, I will bring additional supplies.

- Business cards
- Camera and film or memory stick
- Pens, pencils, and pencil sharpener
- Black markers—fine point and wide point
- Scissors
- Calculator
- Stapler and staples
- Post-its—small, medium, and large
- Tape measures—small and large
- Letter opener
- White multiuse labels—Avery 05450 (3 x 5), Avery 05453 (3 x 4), and Avery 05440 (1.5 x 3)
- Removable See Through Color Dots—Avery 05473
- Index cards, white—small and large
- Small white envelopes
- Label maker – Casio KL820
- Label tapes—9- and 18-millimeter black on white
- Batteries—six in my label maker, six spares, and camera batteries
- Graph paper
- Pad of lined paper
- Hand lotion
- Gloves—light duty and heavy duty
- Band-Aids
- Nail file
- Hair clips

- Tissues
- Breath mints
- Silicone stick—Panef white stick lubricant with silicone
- Day Runner magnetic notepads—for shopping and to-do lists (I offer these to my clients as freebies if I see the need.)
- Standard 1/3-cut manila file folders
- Sample Smead two-ply file folders in a variety of colors
- Classification folders—with pockets and without
- Folder separators—Smead 68021
- Hanging files—Smead V shaped and 1 inch with plastic tabs
- Key tags—Avery 11025

Additional Supplies in My Car

- File boxes
- Storage boxes
- Toolbox—hammer, screwdriver, screws with anchors
- Trash bags
- Extra manila folders
- Furniture sliders for hard flooring and carpeting (www.ezmoves.com are the best)

By now you're probably wondering what size bag will hold all this stuff, right? Believe it or not, I am currently using a diaper bag. I saw it one day while I was shopping. It has so many compartments, inside and out, that it's perfectly suited to carry all the small items I need. Don't worry, it's navy with dark green trim—no cute little characters! It has been a wonderful tool and keeps me very organized.

To find the perfect bag for you, collect all the items you will be carrying in your bag and place them on a table. You can even take a picture or make a list of everything. With the memory—or photo, or list—of all your stuff to refer to, you'll know the perfect-size bag when you see it. This is also a great technique to use whenever you're shopping for client containers.

A final thought: You might want to try maintaining one well-organized workbag that also holds client paperwork, plus one additional personal bag that can hold your wallet, keys, phone, water, lunch or snack, and the like.

Bag Etiquette

Please be organized when you are working with your clients. Don't walk into their home juggling several bags, a bottle of water, some papers, and your purse! Remember, they are watching your every move, evaluating your ability to guide them and assist them in creating organization. If you'd like to continue doing business with them, make sure you continue showing them your talents.

Be consistent about how you keep your items together in clients' homes, too. Always put your keys in the same spot in the bag, keep your bags together, and know where your belongings are at all times. It doesn't say much for you as a professional organizer if clients and potential clients see you slapping your coat pockets, saying, "Now, what *did* I do with those keys?"

It's In The Bag!

Visit www.BalanceAndBeyond.com to see the bag I have developed specifically for Professional Organizers. You can purchase the bag and fill it yourself, or buy it fully stocked with all my recommended supplies. Your one step closer to seeing your first client!

Professionalism

The professional organizing business is built heavily on referrals. And the only way to obtain these referrals is to present yourself as credible, competent, and trustworthy.

Dress and Appearance

For obvious reasons, your wardrobe choices as a professional organizer will be dependent on what you will be doing with clients. For the assessment visit—in which you typically won't be doing any actual organizing—you should be dressed professionally in casual business attire of khakis or other pressed pants. Work session clothing varies according to your clients and the scope of work for the day. For instance, if I'm going to be working in a garage or other environment where the likelihood of getting dirty is high, I wear jeans or black khakis. For interior projects—say, paperwork or kitchens—I typically wear a pair of black pants. I have a great pair that are machine washable and come out wrinkle-free, with a crease down the middle. Black is a good choice because it doesn't show many scuff marks or dirt. When clients realize you've gotten your clothes dirty, they become embarrassed about their "mess" and begin to apologize. Reassure them that these are your work clothes and it's certainly not an issue. Interestingly, black pants do show dust. I sometimes will stand up from having slid under a desk or reached under a dresser only to find dust bunnies attached to me everywhere. Again, remind your clients that you expect a little dust in your job—and it never hurt anyone.

When I'm working in an office environment, I ask my clients what the dress code is and follow it. If the job involves dirty work, I check with clients as to appropriate clothes for work during business hours.

Dressing for your marketing calls and organizer networking is a bit different from organizing. I try to match my surroundings. Business networking is a bit more formal, due the fact that many who attend are heading to an office afterward. I don't want to show up in khakis for this type of event, so business attire is much more appropriate.

When it comes to footwear, choose good supporting shoes or sneakers and keep them in good shape. My first choice is a black or brown flat shoe that is comfortable, flexible, and supportive for the work I'll be doing. It's well worth a trip to a shoe store with professionals who can evaluate your specific needs and guide you to properly fitting shoes. Sneakers are acceptable for garage, outdoor, or basement work as long as they are neat and clean. Don't wear the ones you use on the weekends for gardening!

General Appearance Guidelines

- Wear casual jeans only if you're in a garage or very dirty workplace; dress jeans are fine for most appointments.
- Never wear open-toed shoes or flip-flops!
- Never wear T-shirts with logos or the band you went to see last week.
- Keep your hair up and out of the way.
- No cut-off shirts or pants.
- Keep your makeup and jewelry to the bare minimum.

- Make sure the clothes you choose fit properly. You don't want to be tugging at a shirt that shows more of you than you'd like or pants that seem to work their way down with every move. Remember, you'll be working and moving for most of your session; your clothes should fit comfortably and move easily with you.

Appearance, however, goes beyond just your physical self. Your car, your purse, the bags you carry all have an impact on how you look to your clients and any potential clients. Remember that in a way, you're always being interviewed when others find out what it is you do. Mention that you're a professional organizer and instantly people want to know what your linen closet looks like, or your garage.

Or even your car! I learned this one the hard way. Admittedly, this has always been my trouble spot. I'm not much of a car person, and since I work out of my car—lugging things around, traveling to and fro, eating and drinking as I drive—I have always left the job of car cleaning to my husband. Well, wouldn't you know it: I met a woman at a business meeting who was thinking of hiring me to make a presentation at her office. We happened to walk out to the parking lot together, and as we approached my car, her eyes fell onto my backseat...strewn with what looked like the contents of an entire clothes closet, empty coffee cups, several maps, and the remains of my last organizing session. I never did hear from her about setting up that date. Surprise, surprise!

More Tales from the Car Trenches

Ruthann Betz-Essinger, Just Organized, LLC
"I had a magnetic sign made for the side of my car that had all my business information on it. It has been working to attract clients, but also attracts people interested in seeing just how organized my car is. People are always coming over to peek in the windows and check things out. I soon realized that I needed to keep my car immaculate inside and out all the time. Other than that, it has helped with name recognition—and I did have a woman call me recently who was driving in her car, saw my car, and called me on the spot!"

Respect and Consideration

Having respect for your clients' homes and possessions is crucial in this business. Sarcastic comments about their belongings—"What the heck is this?" or "Why in the world would you buy this?"—or anything that could be considered judgmental is not appropriate. Never throw or toss clients' possessions around, either—not even the ones headed for the garbage. Give everything you handle, from the scraps of paper in a drawer to the antique vase on the mantel, similar respect.

Remember that you're a guest in your clients' homes. Ask before assuming. Never place your water bottle on a piece of furniture, for instance, or stack boxes or bins atop carpets or tables without discussing it with your clients. I once worked with a client sorting out a closet just off the living room. Without thinking, I started putting the contents on the living room carpet. My client was so upset by this that she went out to the garage and brought in clean tarps to put down. After that, every time I pulled something out of the closet, she asked where I was going to put it. It didn't make for a comfortable session!

Communication and Conversations

Communication with your clients should always be professional and courteous. Foul language or off-color humor is never acceptable. Even if clients themselves use inappropriate language, don't take this as a sign that you should, too.

Personal boundaries are critical to the self-employed. It's part of your job to listen to clients tell you stories—about their stuff, about the room, about all sorts of things. But it's not appropriate for you to do the same. It's one thing to share your suggestions with clients, adding the tale of a recent experience you had to support your case; it's another to delve into every detail of the bickering that went on at your

"It's Me!"

I had a client who often left messages on my business phone that started, "Hey Dawn, it's me, I just wanted to . . ." *It's who?* I always wanted to ask.

Make it a habit to use your name and business name when you are leaving a message for a client. "Hello, Janet, it's Dawn from Balance and Beyond. I just wanted . . ." makes for a clear and professional opening.

General Tips for the New Organizer

- When you walk into clients' spaces, it's all new to you, and you'll see it very differently from your clients. Even the smallest of your suggestions may be huge to them.

- What you think is obvious may not be. Remember, not everyone thinks the way you do.

- Verbalize in a nonjudgmental way.

- Ask questions; don't assume.

- Always have your secret-weapon products with you: silicone stick lubricant, furniture sliders, key tags, removable labels, and a label maker. These simple products can make a tremendous impact.

- Research, read, and review prior to each client visit.

- Don't take on something you can't handle. Know when to call in support and when to bow out gracefully.

- Clients come to you when they are ready.

- Maintain your integrity at all times.

- Always be on the lookout for new gadgets. Try them out and know where to get them.

- Keep it simple.

- Offer suggestions and allow clients to choose. If they want to try something you don't recommend, explain your reasons—then allow them to try it their way. If it works, great. If not, they can still opt for one of your suggestions.

- Never stop polishing your skills. Workshops and courses as well as your own clients can offer new perspectives and ideas that keep your business fresh.

- Love what you do.

last family get-together. Even if you think you're just making conversation, it's best to steer clear of any personal issues. Keep it strictly about the client, the work at hand, and any other organizing topic.

And here's another important consideration: It's never appropriate for you to use the names of clients. Before I became an organizer, I was a nurse, and my training comes in quite handy in my new field. In nursing it was of the utmost importance to respect patients' privacy. We could actually get sued if we were heard discussing a patient's private information in an elevator or other public place. You can certainly tell stories to make a point or to share with other organizers. Just make sure they are anonymous ones!

Sharing your experiences in a negative fashion is also a no-no. When folks hear you speaking sarcastically or negatively about another client or situation, they are likely to wonder what you will say about them when they are not around. It's unprofessional and inappropriate. There are many positive, humorous anecdotes you will be able to draw from your client sessions. Do so with a light heart and the intention to inspire those around you, and that's how you'll be received.

Working with Clients

You've been working hard at getting your office space set up, your financial records in order, and your business cards and the look of your company established. You have reviewed your skills, set up training that suits your needs, and have all your supplies ready to go. Next up: clients themselves!

The biggest variable you'll be faced with when it comes to dealing with the clients is, of course, the clients themselves. For better or worse, personalities have a huge impact on the organizing process. Learning some basic psychology will go a long way toward creating great working relationships between you and your clients.

First up, though, let me walk you through some of the more practical client issues you'll be dealing with as you launch your organizing business.

Setting Your Rates

If you are new to business, this step may be uncomfortable for you. How do you establish your rates—and, even more important, how do you convey these rates to a potential client with confidence? I have provided a formula below to help you establish what your rates will be. There are also industry standards. Do you have competitors in your area? If so, find out what they charge. It will give you an idea of what the market will bear in your particular location. I'm not saying that what one organizer charges is the fee you should set for yourself, but it's a good reference point to be aware of.

The Rate Formula

I briefly discussed the formula for setting your rates in chapter 1, but it's worth repeating here in more detail. First, figure out how much you'd like to make this year working with individual clients. Then decide how many hours a week you will be out of your house with those clients. Multiply the hours per week

On the Road Again

I have very rarely charged for travel miles or time and here is why: I hate to travel! I typically won't take a client if the client is further than forty-five minutes from where I live. My policy, if and when I do travel, is that I charge half my hourly rate for anything above forty-five minutes in one direction. For instance, if it takes me one hour to get there, then there and back is thirty minutes total over my allotted forty-five minutes each way, so I bill my client one quarter hour of time. Of course, if you're in need of clients, this policy may be something to wave. Just be sure you want to do that. I will follow a client that has moved for a period of adjustment. I had a client, a very good paying client, who moved and was an hour and a half (each way) away. I told her I would not charge her for the first month after she moved for travel but after that I would. She quickly realized that she needed to find someone closer, and I helped her with that process.

by the number of weeks you want to work per year—keeping in mind holidays and vacations. You may decide, for instance, that you'd like to work 45 weeks per year, and that you're willing to work with clients 20 hours a week. Your total number of paying hours is then 900 (45 x 20 = 900). If an annual income of $50,000 is your target, then divide that by your 900 hours—in this case giving you an hourly rate of $55. That's what you'll charge your clients.

This is, of course, a very simplistic way of thinking about rates, since it doesn't take into account any expenses you'll incur. Look at the yearly expenses I estimated for you under "Operating Costs" in chapter 1. This is information you may want to include in your rate calculation. Let's say you want to earn $50,000 and know your expenses to be approximately $10,000 a year. Take $60,000 and divide by 900 hours, which gives you a rate of $67 per hour. Here are the specifics:

> $60,000 desired annual income
> 20 hours per week with clients
> 20 hours x 45 weeks (taking into account sick days, vacations, and
>   holidays) = 900 hours per year
> $60,000 ÷ 900 hours = $67 per hour

Keep in mind that you may well not have exactly twenty hours of work every week; the actual total could be more or less. These figures are a ballpark estimate, and if you're counting on this income to maintain a household, you will need to take a more comprehensive approach to calculating your rates and/or evaluating hours. Another thing to remember is that you don't want to go too far below the average rates for professional organizers. If you go low, believe it or not clients will think they aren't getting quality. If you go too high, however, they might think you're overpriced. Keep within the range of $55 and $150 for private individual clients and you're good.

Don't Nickel-and-Dime Your Clients

Yes, you want to charge clients for products purchased. Yes, clients should pay if you stay longer or work outside of session hours and have agreed on it. However, if you've stocked your bag with a few items (labels, index cards, stick lubricant, etc.) and use them, it's a part of the cost of doing business. Recently I was working on organizing a kitchen with a very good client. We found a container of extra keys. She starts rattling off which ones were for which (as if anyone else would know this!). I went directly to my bag and pulled out my key tags (Avert 11026) and started putting a tag on each key, even the ones she didn't know. She said, "Wow, where did you find those?" I explained I had them in my bag for just this occasion. She was so excited about something so small. I think of it as a marketing expense. She immediately said, "You are *good*."

Creating Package Rates

When I'd been in business for about a year, one of my clients asked if she could get a discount by paying up front for a block of hours. I told her that I didn't have anything like this, but I could put some thought into it and discuss it at our next visit. I created two packages: a twenty-hour package with a 10 percent discount and a forty-hour package with a 15 percent discount. I chose twenty and forty because my typical session is four hours long, which equates to five and ten sessions, respectively. Both packages needed to be paid for in full up front. Well, at our very next session, this client handed me a check for a twenty-hour package, and within two months all my current and new clients were on packages. I would have never thought clients would pay up front for services, but they certainly did—and it was great. I didn't have to discuss or take payment at each visit; all I did was review the hours on the work record. To this day, most of my clients choose packages.

These package rates provided another benefit. It was always a challenge to handle a client who canceled an appointment the day before our scheduled visit. Even though I had discussed the cancellation policy, I never wanted to alienate a client. It's not like I would send an invoice for time we didn't spend together. It was much easier to charge hours. For instance, the client purchased a twenty-hour package, and has sixteen hours left. The client canceled at the last minute for an appointment. I charged half our hours, so the client now only has fourteen hours left. This was something that seemed much easier for me to do. I can honestly say I've only done it a handful of times, but it certainly comes in handy when you have a client who perpetually cancels.

Client Forms

When working with clients, my experience is that keeping forms to a minimum is key. Again, clients are calling you because they have too much clutter and can't find things. The more stuff you give them, the more chances they have of losing it. Keep a folder containing the pertinent forms with you and review it at the close of business with clients on each visit.

Client Intake Form

The first form you'll need when working with clients is the intake form. When you get a call from potential clients, use this form to record all the pertinent information about them and their organizing needs. I usually grab one of these while I'm on the phone with the client and write down keys words that I hear, along with any specifics they share with me—children's names, problem areas, and the like. A sample of the form I use is on page 98.

Assessment Visit/Working Agreement

One of the more important forms you will create is the agreement between you and clients. It will set the expectations for the work you do. It can be a very formal contract or as informal as you like. I strongly recommend that it be written, however. The Working Agreement includes your cancellations policy, appointment confirmation phone call policy, scope of work, rates, travel reimbursement statement, and anything else specific to your work. I have chosen to combine my Assessment Visit and Working Agreement into one form (see page 99). Later on, when we talk about the assessment visit, I will show you how this form looks once it's completed.

Work Record

This form is where you track the hours worked and progress made at each work session. To give clients a copy of it would be self-defeating. They are usually over-burdened with paperwork as it is; keeping track of yet one more piece of paper is a nuisance. Instead, complete this at your first visit and let the clients know you will have it in their file to review at each visit. It lists payments made, dates and hours, and a brief description of the work completed. I have never had a client challenge hours or payments. I believe it's because I make it a point to review both at each visit. A sample of this form is on page 100.

[Your Logo Here]
CLIENT INTAKE FORM

Name: _____

Date: _____

Address: _____

Phone: _____

How did they hear about us: _____ _____

General phone intake: *Here is where you write down parts of your initial conversation with clients. Do they have children? Do they work or are they stay-at-home parents? What's the reason for their call? What's their primary area of interest? Any information that allows you to get to know the client would be captured here.*

You can also jot down what you've discussed: rates, packages, time frames, and so forth. You will review this with them at your assessment visit.

If you schedule an assessment visit at this point, write it down here and in your calendar.

Directions: _____

_____

_____

General client/family description: *This is where you write down your impressions after your assessment visit. When they call back to schedule future appointments, you'll want to recall any conversations you had at your assessment.*

_____

_____

_____

Plan: *Record your initial plan for the clients. At this point you will have left an assessment form with them, but you need to recall what you wrote down. You can also record their available days and times here.*

_____

_____

_____

Visit www.BalanceAndBeyond.com for downloadable version.

[Your Logo Here]
ASSESSMENT VISIT/WORKING AGREEMENT

Name: _____

Date: _____

Address: _____

Phone: _____

Estimate of work schedule:

_____   _____

_____   _____

_____   _____

_____   _____

_____   Totals: _____

Hourly and package rates:

Tips to get started:

_____   _____

_____   _____

_____   _____

Plan of action: _____

Working agreement:

Phone call confirmation: Unless otherwise stated, I will not call to confirm appointments. If you need to change or reschedule your appointment time, it is your responsibility to contact the office and do so.

Cancellation policy: Cancellation of a scheduled appointment with less than 48 hours' notice will be billed at 50 percent of the agreed-upon rate or time scheduled.

Travel rates: Travel greater than 45 minutes in either direction will be billed at 50 percent of the agreed-upon rate.

Business Name   **Phone**   **Website**

Visit www.BalanceAndBeyond.com for downloadable version.

[Your Logo Here]
WORK RECORD

Client name: _____

Address: _____

Phone number: _____

Payment record:

Rates quoted to client:

Package hours: _____

Date: _____ Time: _____ Project: _____ # Hrs. Wrkd: _____ # Hrs. Left: _____

Date: _____ Time: _____ Project: _____ # Hrs. Wrkd: _____ # Hrs. Left: _____

Date: _____ Time: _____ Project: _____ # Hrs. Wrkd: _____ # Hrs. Left: _____

Date: _____ Time: _____ Project: _____ # Hrs. Wrkd: _____ # Hrs. Left: _____

Date: _____ Time: _____ Project: _____ # Hrs. Wrkd: _____ # Hrs. Left: _____

Date: _____ Time: _____ Project: _____ # Hrs. Wrkd: _____ # Hrs. Left: _____

Date: _____ Time: _____ Project: _____ # Hrs. Wrkd: _____ # Hrs. Left: _____

Date: _____ Time: _____ Project: _____ # Hrs. Wrkd: _____ # Hrs. Left: _____

Date: _____ Time: _____ Project: _____ # Hrs. Wrkd: _____ # Hrs. Left: _____

Date: _____ Time: _____ Project: _____ # Hrs. Wrkd: _____ # Hrs. Left: _____

Date: _____ Time: _____ Project: _____ # Hrs. Wrkd: _____ # Hrs. Left: _____

Visit www.BalanceAndBeyond.com for downloadable version.

Homework

One of my newest forms is the "homework" sheet. It may include items to be purchased, files to be purged, items to be donated, decisions about keeping or not keeping a particular item, paperwork, talking to a spouse regarding something, etc. It includes whatever steps the client and I have identified as work that the client can accomplish prior to the next visit. At the start of the next visit I review the client's homework. If the client completed it, great, we've got a jumping off point. If not, it's a great time to have a conversation about why some projects may take longer to accomplish than originally predicted, particularly since we cannot move forward without these pieces completed (if that's the case). Either way, it's good to have a way to keep the client active between visits and keep progress happening.

Sample Homework Checklist

Homework

Date

Next Visit:

- ☐
- ☐
- ☐
- ☐
- ☐
- ☐
- ☐
- ☐
- ☐
- ☐
- ☐
- ☐
- ☐

Invoice

I use invoices mostly for corporate clients. Once they have approved a proposal (I'll show this to you shortly), I complete and send an invoice for the proposed services. I have occasionally used invoices with private or individual clients if their employer is paying for my services, or they have a home business that will be covering the bill.

I've included my own invoice on the next page as a sample for you. You can also use the invoices provided with any financial accounting software you might be using, which automatically record each invoice for you. If you use the following form, I suggest you make the invoice number the day service began. Then all your invoices will be in numerical order from the beginning of the year.

Receipts

When I started out in this business, I bought one of those receipt books available at any office supply store, expecting to give clients one after each payment. I offered it to every client when they paid. After several months went by and I hadn't written out a single receipt, I realized that no one wanted yet another piece of paper to clutter up their space. I pitched the receipt book and never looked back.

Proposals

I've found that I only rarely need to make formal proposals when I'm working with private clients. They simply agree to my initial assessment and fees, and I'm off and running. Any additional work I'll be doing with the client is outlined in my Assessment Form/Working Agreement; if they agree, I'm all set.

When you enter the world of bosses, committees, and corporate structure, however, things change. You must be prepared to submit a proposal to be discussed, reviewed, and (hopefully) approved. In general there are two types of corporate proposals: one for organizing, the other for speaking or training. Any proposal you make should include the following:

[Your Logo Here]

INVOICE

Date: _____

Client: _____

Address: _____

Invoice #: _____

Description of services: _____

_____

_____

Fee: _____

Total: $ _____

Payment terms: *Payment is due first day of service (larger packages may be split up into two payments, if you'd like).*

Congratulations on your commitment to getting organized. We're happy to be assisting you along your journey!

Thank you,

Your name
Business name
Business address
Phone number

Visit www.BalanceAndBeyond.com for downloadable version.

Proposal for Organizing Services

- The problem, as identified by you and the contact person
- The goal, as identified by you and the contact person
- An estimate of your hours and schedule
- Your payment schedule
- Your cancellation policy

Proposal for a Speaking Engagement or Training Program

- The title of your presentation
- The length of your presentation
- A list of supplies you will need
- A list of supplies you will provide
- The cost of this work
- Your payment schedule
- Your cancellation policy

A sample proposal is included on the next page for your reference.

Keep your proposals simple and easy to understand. They should be one or two pages at the most. Remember, you want to set an example of simplicity and organization at all times, so make your communication clear and concise.

● ● ●

And there you have it: client paperwork in a nutshell. Pretty simple, right? That's the way we like it. Of course, you can get more detailed with each of these forms, but why? As long as you cover the important information, you're good. As you move forward with your organizing practice, you can adjust these forms to include additional information as you see fit.

Please visit my website (www.balanceandbeyond.com) to download blank versions of these forms for you to use.

Answering the Call

You've spoken at some local club meetings, you've run an ad or two, you've attended a networking meeting or perhaps listed yourself in a local registry of services—and suddenly the call comes in. Someone is interested in your services. What do you say? How do you get started? What in the world do you do now? First, take a breath and relax. This is what you've been waiting for. These clients have found you because

[Your Logo Here]

January 20, 2011

Dear Mary,

It was a pleasure speaking with you last week. I look forward to working with you and your group. I've put together a proposal for the program we discussed. Please call me with any questions.

Tentative presentation dates: April 14 or June 30. Time: 12:30–3:00 p.m.

Title: 4 Steps to Organizing Anything

Description: Learn the 4 Steps to organizing anything. From the trunk of your car to your office, you can learn how to systematically plow through chaos with ease. Learn how to create an environment that reflects who you are and what's important to you. This workshop is interactive, fun, and informative. You get hands-on experience and leave with a written plan for your number one problem area.

Supplies I'll need from you:

Overhead projector

Eraser board

Classroom-style or U-shaped setup

Supplies I'll provide:

Handouts

Demonstration materials

Cost: One 2?-hour workshop @ $XXX/hour = $XXX.00

Payment of 50 percent is required to hold the date. The balance is due on the presentation date.

Cancellation policy: The deposit is held. A new, mutually agreed-upon date is scheduled within one year from original date or the deposit is forfeited.

Please call me with any questions. I look forward to hearing from you!

Thank you,

Jane Doe

they are ready to make a change, and they are willing to pay you to make it happen, so rest assured—all you have to do now is find out what exactly they need help with.

The first conversation may go something like this:

Caller: Hi, my name is Sandy and I saw your ad. I'm interested in talking more about what you do.

You: That's great, I'm glad you called. Tell me, what about the ad caught your attention?

Caller: Well, the whole ad really, the organizing, paperwork, I feel like I need it all. I moved into this house three years ago and I feel like I still haven't unpacked and gotten things organized. It's just getting to a point where I'm exhausted and I think I need help.

You: What's the one area that feels most out of control?

Caller: I guess it would be my office, or the paperwork that I'm dealing with, but that seems like it's just the tip of the iceberg.

You: Well, I can tell you that you're not alone. Especially after a move, it seems like life moves very quickly; getting settled can be tough. I can tell you a little bit about how we work.

Caller: That would be great.

You: The first step is an initial assessment. This usually takes about an hour to an hour and a half. We tour your space and discuss the areas that you feel aren't working for you. We talk about what specific problems you might be having and what it is you hope to create. I give you tips and techniques along the way that I can immediately see would make a difference, and when we're done, I sit down and create a plan to help get you organized. I can give you approximate time frames for each area we tour and then we can talk about how to get started.

Caller: That sounds great. How much does that cost?

You: The initial assessment costs $XXX. That includes the tips and techniques and specific steps to make immediate changes. If you sign up for an organizing package while I'm there, I discount the price of the assessment as well.

Caller: How does it work when you come to visit?

You: Well, we work side by side on particular tasks, and then I give you homework to complete between each session. I suggest making regularly scheduled visits to keep on track. The more consistent we are about appointments, the more quickly we make progress. I work in four-hour blocks of time and have hourly rates and discounted package rates.

Caller: I love the way it sounds and I'm very excited. Let's schedule an initial assessment.

You: Absolutely, let me open my calendar and we'll look at dates.

And that's how a professional organizer gets started. If you start getting nervous or flustered, remember that clients call you because they are interested in your services. If you listen closely, you will hear what they need. The reason you went into this business is because you like to help people solve their organizing problems, so let your instincts guide you. Talk with callers as you would a friend. Most potential clients can see through a sales pitch, and your intention is not to sell them, but to let them know you can help.

A Mess All Their Own

So often people just need to be seen exactly where they are, with all the mess they've gotten themselves into before they can move beyond it. As an organizer you get to witness peoples' journeys and thus contribute to their inner healing process. This is a great honor full of its own rewards, but the only way to excel at this part of the job is to heal and grow yourself and to consciously deal with your own "stuff." This is not always easy, but it too carries its own rewards. Kathy Smyly Miller, www.kathysmylymiller.com

Discussing Your Rates

The toughest conversation to have with potential clients is the one about money. It will take some practice, but it is very important to get comfortable with your rates and with discussing them. You can practice with family or friends by doing some role-playing, or you could write yourself a little script to use when potential clients call. It may feel very awkward at first, but the more you do it, the easier it gets. After all, you've spent a good amount of time determining your rates and evaluating your skills. Hopefully you have apprenticed, been coached, or polished your skills to a level you're confident with. It's important now not to underestimate your value and the experience you bring to the organizing job. It is your job to set the bar and to perform to those standards.

Frequently Asked Questions—and How to Answer Them

Some particular questions seem to come up again and again when organizers talk to potential clients. Here's a primer in what to expect—and what to do:

- **Do you have any clients I can talk to?** Your answer to this should always be yes. Whether they're paying or nonpaying clients, you should have a list of at least three or four individuals who are willing to speak about your skills as an organizer. These may include relatives or friends whom you've helped, or perhaps previous clients. Regardless, if prospective clients are interested in checking your references, they should be offered several names. Contact anyone you have done work with and ask them if they would be willing to speak with new prospects. Most friends and family members will agree, and most clients are willing to accommodate you if you ask. Keep this list handy so that you can provide it to the prospective clients immediately.

- **How many clients have you had?** Good question. What if this is your first client? Well, again, you should have a list of family and friends for whom you have done work. You can count anyone you have done work with or for as a client. So count them up and use that number. Your response may end up something like this: "I'm not sure of the exact number—somewhere between ten and twenty. What I can tell you is that I've been organizing since as far back as I can remember, and although I may be new in business, I'm confident that the work we do together will be beneficial. I can help you get things in order quickly and efficiently."

- **Where did you learn how to do this?** Always be truthful when you're talking with clients; never put your integrity in question. When people asked me this question, I was able to cite the work I had done with another organizer as part of my training, but I also relied heavily on my previous work experience and the education I gave myself reading and researching. My answer went something like this: "That's a great question; I sometimes wonder where I learned this myself. What I can tell you is that I recently worked side by side with a seasoned organizer for four months and have read more than seventy-five books on the subject. I am passionate about the work that I do and pride myself on hitting the mark when it comes to designing systems specific to each client's needs."

■ **Have you ever worked with a client like me?** This is a common question. People seem to think that their mess is unique and unlike anything I've ever seen. I tell them, "Each client is different, but I haven't met a mess yet that I couldn't handle. Remember, I love what I do—and I say, the bigger the better!" They usually laugh and respond with, "Well, let's wait and see," or something similar.

■ **What if you can't help me?** Folks usually ask this because they're afraid. They may be afraid to spend money only to learn they're a lost cause; or perhaps they fear that the work you do won't fix the problem. I talk with such clients and reassure them: "Half the battle is making the decision to call in support; the other half is for us to tackle the problems together. Once we've met and completed the initial assessment, we'll sit and talk about where you're at and what you can reasonably expect from our working together. I will let you know where we will be able to make big changes, and if there are areas that will need to be addressed differently, we will find the right resources."

■ **Do you work on weekends?** The answer to this question is more about you than anything else. If you have made up your mind not to work weekends, then the answer is simple, "No, I do not." If you are more flexible and are willing to work weekends if necessary, you can say, "I occasionally work weekends if that's the only time a client can meet me. My weekends are limited, though, and we would need to look at the calendar to see when would be good." If you are not opposed to weekends at all, then "Sure, weekends are fine with me," would be your response.

■ **Do you actually do the work with me?** Answer: "Yes, all the organizing we do will be with your input and direct involvement. You need to be able to function in the systems we set up, and without your input that just won't happen." If clients tell you that they don't know if they have the time to get so involved, remind them that their commitment will be well worth it in the long run. I let them know that I will make every effort to work within their schedules.

■ **What if my spouse/child/colleague wants to work with us?** The more the merrier, I say! Let clients know that as long as the other folks involved will not cause friction, it would be great to have them on board. If the client has an argumentative spouse, of course, it may be unproductive to involve him or her. Be forewarned: You are not a referee, but you may find yourself wanting to blow a whistle! As the organizer, you need to monitor the project's progress and address any situation that may be compromising the progress.

■ **Is it just about throwing things out?** This is an easy one. "No, it's not. We may identify items that you'd be willing to part with, but organizing is about discovering what's important to you and finding ways to make a new system work."

■ **What should I do to prepare for your visit?** Nothing. You want to see the clients' space exactly the way they deal with it on a day-to-day basis. Every pile tells a story, and you want to hear the entire story.

Your Initial-Call Hit List

- Ask how they heard about you.

- Get their name, phone number, address, and e-mail.

- Thank them for calling.

- Tell them not to clean up before you visit.

This list is nowhere near complete; clients are forever coming up with new stumpers. Be as prepared as you can, but ultimately there's nothing wrong with replying, "That's a good question—I've never been asked that before. I'll have to give it some thought." The thing to remember is that clients are getting ready to invite you into their world of chaos. They ask questions not only to get the answers, but more importantly to get to know you a bit better and make sure they want to let you in!

The Assessment Visit

The assessment visit is critical in your relationship with clients. It is your first meeting face-to-face, a time when you will be sizing each other up. You will check on things like your safety (including the neighborhood you are in), who else is in the home, and any environmental situations that might be harmful—mold, for instance, or rooms under construction. You will also be evaluating the size of the job, client readiness, and project needs. Clients, on the other hand, will be asking themselves: *Can this organizer help me? Can I trust this person? Do I feel comfortable with this stranger traipsing through my house?* Clearly, your assessment visit will have great impact on whether you land the clients.

Depending on whom you talk to in the organizing world, you will get varying opinions on whether to charge for this visit, or not. I have always charged for my assessment visit and strongly advise you do as well. I spend a good ninety minutes with clients, and in that time I offer quick tips and techniques that will help them make immediate changes to different areas of their home or office space. Another reason I charge is that I want to weed out any potential window shoppers. My time is valuable, and if I'm out doing initial assessments and not getting paid, how will I earn an income? I have found that if clients are willing to pay for the assessment, they are generally ready to get to work.

One option is to waive the fee if clients sign up for a package on the spot. I've done that in the past, but sometimes I feel like I'm putting too much pressure on people to sign up. On the other hand, I feel like I am not rewarding them for signing up if I don't offer them something, so I have recently started discounting the assessment visit if they sign up for services. This seems to work well.

What to Bring

So you've scheduled the assessment visit, and today's the day. Here's what you'll need to bring with you on your first appointment:

- Client Intake Form
- Client folder
- Directions to the clients' house
- Map/GPS
- Your workbag
- A printout of your current rates
- Business cards
- Assessment Visit/Working Agreement form
- Digital camera
- A bottle of water
- Confidence

What to Expect

You have all the tools you need, and you're on your way. You've gotten directions from either the clients or a computer program, and you have your trusty map with you. How much time should you give yourself to get there? My suggestion is fifteen to twenty minutes more than you think you'll need. If you get there early, great—sit in your car around the corner, review the Client Intake Form, take deep cleansing breaths, and recall why you're doing this work in the first place—because you love it and you know you can help people. If you run into traffic or get a little lost, however, you still have some time to spare.

If you've set up an exact time for the appointment, be punctual. It's not a good start to the relationship if you're running late, especially for an organizer! So watch your time. My recommendation is to be flexible about your first appointment time. You might, for example, tell the clients you will arrive between two and two thirty. This way, you have accounted for any unusual traffic issues or direction problems you may encounter. Subsequent appointments can be more precise.

Ready? Now...go knock on the door.

The clients who answer will likely be nervous. Remember, you have asked them to *not* clean or pick up anything because you need to see their space as they do. Now they are letting you, a total stranger, into their home. It can understandably be a bit overwhelming.

Introduce yourself and tell them you're happy to be there. They won't know what to do next—whether to start touring you through their space or to offer you a drink. First suggest that you get settled—at the kitchen table or a desk area, perhaps—so you can put down your bag and get out your notepad.

Because you're working with clients on such a personal level, they sometimes feel obliged to offer you food or drink. Thank them for the offer, but tell them you have brought water for yourself. Bringing your own water shows clients that there is no need for them to take care of you. It reinforces the fact that you are there to serve them and support them.

I once accepted an offer for a cup of coffee from a client. Seems harmless, right? Well, she happened to have soy milk that day, so I used it. She noticed that I used the soy milk and for every appointment from that point on, no matter what I said, she made sure she had soy milk available. She even sent her husband out for soy milk one morning before I arrived, telling him he needed to get it for the organizer! Having your own supplies will prevent this sort of awkwardness.

With your notepad and client file in hand, take a minute to review the conversation you initially had over the phone. You should reiterate to the clients what their initial concerns were and remind them that you're here to help with these issues. You want clients as comfortable as possible with you in these first few minutes so they can be more at ease during the tour.

You want to instill in them the sense that you are there to support them and not to judge them. Here's a tip toward that end: *Don't* comment on what a beautiful neighborhood they live in, or how nice their house is. I know this sounds strange, but such comments may actually intimidate them. They may be reluctant to show you spaces that aren't so attractive—thinking, perhaps, *Well, this room might be nice but wait till she sees my office.* Instead, be sure your comments as you enter the home relate to why you are here and how glad you are they called. You might say, "The directions you gave were excellent," or "I've been looking forward to meeting you after our phone conversation the other day," or "I'm excited to get started." Sometimes it's hard to make small talk, but please be wary of making any judgments, good or bad.

After you've had a few minutes with the clients and hopefully created a bit of a comfort zone, it's time to go on the tour. "Where should we start?" ask the clients. You can respond by suggesting a particular area, or you can say, "Let's start right here. Tell me about this room." Now is the time to pose your assessment questions. What's working? What's not? Face into whatever room you are in and ask. Continue asking as you walk through the house. You will be taking notes and listening very carefully to what they are telling you. Here are some of the questions you can ask during your tour:

Tour Questions

- What's working?
- What's not working?
- What activities take place in this room?
- What items do you need here?
- What do you think is the problem?
- What is your dream outcome for this space?

Some clients will sing like jailbirds, telling you their life stories and the detailed history of each item in the room. Others will tell you all about the other occupants and how they are creating the mess; still others will mumble and sink deeper and deeper into a defeated posture as you walk through each room. Your goal for the tour is to elicit the information you need to provide them with a good-faith estimate of what it will take to get these spaces in order. Keep this in mind, and try not to get too wrapped up in any one area or topic. You are looking to get a general idea of the problem in all the areas you are touring. You may start to see a pattern—too much stuff, not enough storage, no systems in place. That's exactly the kind of information you're looking for right now. Keeping things general like this will get you through the assessment in a timely manner. Once you and the clients are together digging into the mess, you will be getting more specific about every item.

Keep your assessment moving along. If you notice you're running long, work on picking up the pace without rushing things. Base your timing in each room on the size of the house. Here is a typical breakdown of an assessment visit:

10 minutes: Arrive, get settled, and get reacquainted.
45-55 minutes: Tour the space.
10 minutes: Complete the assessment form.
15-20 minutes: Wrap up and schedule the next appointment.
Total: Approximately 80–95 minutes.

After touring the house and returning to the kitchen table, or somewhere else where you can write up your notes, ask the clients if you can have a few minutes to be alone with your thoughts. Clients will usually go get something to drink or go to the bathroom. They are usually a little overwhelmed at this point, too; the break is good for both of you. You, in the meantime, will complete the Assessment Visit/Working Agreement form that you will leave behind. On it, you offer estimates for how long it would take to get each space or room in order, provide a written list of your rates, write down all the tips and suggestions you made as you took the tour, and offer tips on how to get started. You also give them their first homework assignment.

What's that? you're wondering. Here are some ideas for initial homework assignments:

- Take before pictures.
- Find local donation sites.
- Sit in the space you will be organizing and begin to think of your dream space and what it might feel like.
- Start a notebook of ideas or thoughts about the organizing process—the good, the bad, and the ugly.

When clients return, again, remind them that you are happy they called and that you see lots of potential for their space. Review each area of the assessment form with them. When you get to your estimate, give them a number of hours for each room or area that you assessed, then total this number for an overall estimate. For instance, it may take four to six hours for the living room, six to eight hours for the kitchen, and eight to ten hours for the garage; the total would be eighteen to twenty-four hours.

Seek and Ye Shall *Find*

During your assessment visit, you'll want to see the volume of what's stuffed in those cabinets, crammed in those drawers, hidden behind closed doors. Always ask permission first. Put your hand on a particular cabinet and say, "May I open and see?" Or, "Can we take a look?" This is important when it comes to giving clients a good faith estimate of time. The first couple of doors and drawers may be awkward, and then it gets easier.

I then ask what two areas, if we could get them in order immediately, would give them the most satisfaction. They choose their two, and you look at the hours you have estimated and say, "I estimate fourteen to eighteen hours to get those two areas in order." I always emphasize that these are estimates only, and the actual work may take more or less time depending on how slowly or quickly they make decisions and whether they choose to do additional work, on their own or with their family, between our sessions.

Turning to rates, I tell clients they can pay as we go; however, this is where I typically suggest a package of hours versus paying the hourly organizing rate. I point out the discount if they do this and the fact that their total number of hours to get their home or office in order is (say) thirty-nine hours, so the package may be the way to go.

Next, I review how the schedule works. I tell them that I like to work in blocks of four or more hours because I have found this to be the minimum time it takes to make good progress. I have found that shorter periods give very little actual working time, taking into account the time it takes to ramp up as well as the cleanup time.

I once had a client who insisted that she could only meet for two hours at a time; I was new in business and didn't want to lose her, so I agreed. After several sessions of two hours each, with many interruptions, we were well off the estimates I had created. The client was not satisfied with our progress, and I had very little to rebut with since I had agreed to these conditions. I am now strict about the work sessions that I establish with the client.

I highly recommend setting a standing appointment, if possible. You might, for example, schedule Tuesday from 1 to 5 p.m. each week for five weeks. This creates a momentum, and the project is accomplished more efficiently because there is a decrease in "backslide." I almost always insist on a standing appointment schedule when it comes to larger projects or paperwork issues or if clients have complicated schedules.

Estimating the Job

Let's go back a bit to the part of the assessment where you estimate the hours it will take to complete each area or project. How do you determine the number of hours it will take to get a room in order? This is a bit tricky when you first get started, but the more experience you have, the easier it becomes. There are a couple of items to keep in mind.

First, the job usually takes longer then you think it will. The reason is that as an organizer, you estimate a job based on what you would do in the room with your expertise; however, your clients will be processing and making decisions at a different pace. You must accommodate this in your estimate. Yes, it's your job to keep clients moving at a reasonable pace, but you cannot force the issue, so you essentially have to assess the clients as well as the project when you're making an initial estimate. Are they quick to make decisions or do they seem to struggle with each one? I suggest that you build some additional hours in to your estimates, especially when the process is new to you. If your first thought is that you're looking at six or seven hours of work, I recommend writing down eight to ten. If you come in under the hours estimated, great!

The second thing to keep in mind when estimating a job is that one room or area typically leads into another, and sometimes you can get a bit off track. Let's say you are working in a playroom and determine that there are too many toys to properly store there. You suggest creating space in a basement to store rotating toys. You may then choose to help the clients set up a basic system of basement toy storage before you begin taking them out of the playroom. The solution could be as simple as cardboard boxes, labeled with the contents, located in a particular section of the basement. Still, no matter how simple it is, setting up your new system will take time away from the playroom. You could ask your clients to move the toys to the basement themselves for you to deal with later. However, I have found that the more systems you set up along the way, the better the project unfolds. Leaving a client with a basement or storage room full of chaos is not what you want, even if you do create an awesome playroom. You want every part of your process with them to

In Over Your Head

When will you know if you're in over your head? As a new organizer, you may not know until, well, you're in over your head! If you watch the show hoarders, you'll see the extreme cases of this profession. If you enter a home that looks like one of those, my suggestion…help them find a resource. You can remain on the team, but don't try this on your own; you'll be sorry. First, the sheer magnitude of "stuff" will break your back, and second, the client's mental preparation (or lack there of) will break your spirit. Any time a client is being forced, demanded, or required to organize, it will be an uphill battle every step of the way. As a new organizer you don't have what it takes to tackle this. Find a seasoned organizer, one who specializes in hoarding and know that you've assisted the client in the best way possible.

What if it doesn't look like that, but you find yourself being swallowed up in the process? Finish the work session as scheduled and reach out for help. Take pictures if possible to share with a more seasoned organizer. I have done many consultations with new organizers over the phone to coach them through a rough patch or two. Believe me, after you've gone through this once, you are a better "estimator" of what a job will take. Sometimes you just need to be in over your head to discover your strengths and weaknesses and move on.

be a good experience; it will encourage them to continue working with you and to feel that you are taking the whole picture into account.

Creating time estimates is a learning process, but go with your instincts. With practice, you'll be able to quickly and accurately estimate any space.

Signing Clients Up

Your assessment is complete, you've calculated your good-faith estimate of time, and you're ready to sign the clients on. When it comes to selling your service, there are many schools of thought. I have never been interested in "selling someone"; I believe that it has to be clients' choice whether they're going to commit. There's little worse than having reluctant clients who feel they were sold or convinced to do something they weren't ready for. I simply explain my rates and Working Agreement, and talk about the benefits they will see and feel. Again, I firmly believe that clients come to me when they're ready; they love to pay me good money for what I love to do. Armed with this philosophy, there is no reason to sell my services or myself.

I believe that if there is any selling to be done, it has been in the process up to now. How I listen, how I provide information, how I conduct myself during the assessment...all of this is part of the selling process. By the time clients are ready to commit to working with me, there is very little I need to do other than discuss the benefits for them and the pricing.

As we've discussed, negotiating rates can be tricky, especially for new business owners. Even if you've sold products or services before, discussing rates for your services can be unnerving. The assessment form included here includes a spot to write in your current rates; this way you can simply point to the numbers, taking clients' attention off you for a minute. Remember, package rates are a great way to offer a discount—and who doesn't love to feel like they are getting a deal?

Here's another tip for getting comfortable with pricing: Practice saying your rates out loud with a friend or spouse before you go on a visit. You want to be able to discuss fees without tripping over the numbers and words. Here are some scripts to get you started:

- "My rate is $65 an hour. To make the best use of our time, I work in blocks of four hours at a time. Sometimes we can work longer, but four hours is the minimum."
- "My rate is $65 an hour, but I recommend a package of twenty [or forty, or whatever package you have] hours to get you started and let you take advantage of my package discount."

Collecting Your Fee

For the first five years I was in business, I accepted checks and cash only, regardless of the size of the project or fee. Recently I have started to accept credit cards through my website. I collect the fee for the initial assessment at the time of the assessment visit. If a client wants to take advantage of my discounted assessment rate, then they must pay for a package at the time of the assessment. If clients choose to pay hourly, then I collect payment at the end of each session. I *highly* recommend against billing clients for your services—this can easily get you into trouble if they fall behind on their payments. If you don't want to be in a position where you're asking multiple times for a client to pay you, then don't get there in the first place! Billing clients may work elsewhere in business, but for some reason it gets sticky here. Trust me!

The Tip Sheet

I leave all clients with the following tip sheet whether they start service with me or not. I put it on my letterhead so it has my company information on it.

My Favorite Organizing Tips

Mail: Have a basket, bin, or other decorative object to catch mail as it comes into the house. Locate this by the door where the mail comes in. If there's room, have a separate mail bin or baskets for each member of your household. It makes distributing information easier. Plan to review mail at a predetermined time in your weekly schedule.

Closets: Whenever you remove an item from a hanger, put the hanger in a basket. When you get ready to do laundry, bring the basket for easy "out-of-dryer-onto-hanger" action!

Time: Learn how long it *really* takes you to do your routine tasks and chores, like getting ready in the morning, driving to work, emptying the dishwasher, getting the kids up and dressed for school, laundry, grocery shopping, and so on. This will help in organizing your daily and weekly schedule. If you assume it takes you ten minutes to get ready and leave the house, but in reality it takes thirty, you'll be twenty minutes late for whatever is next on your schedule, and so on for the remainder of the day.

Photos: One way to sort backlogs of photos is to collect shoe boxes or plastic containers and write a year on each one. Sort photos into their correct year. This can be done in brief sessions—even fifteen minutes a night will make a difference by the end of a week. Along the way you can eliminate any duplicates, ugly photos, blurry images, and so forth. Once the pictures are sorted by year, decide how you want to sort them further. Chronologically? By event? Then you can choose how you want to store and/or display them. You will have a better idea of what size album, box, or frames you'll need. Two good resources for storage and display ideas are Exposures (800-222-4947; www.exposuresonline.com) and Century Photo Direct (800-767-0777; www.centuryphoto.com).

Family meetings: Designate an hour a week to synchronize your family. Everyone brings their calendars, to-do lists, and schedules to the table. Spend the time reviewing the events for the upcoming week, expectations for dinners, chores, et cetera. After you have met with your entire family (thirty minutes), parents should meet to review plans (thirty minutes). Try this…you'll be amazed at the incredible results for just one hour of investment time!

Store it where you use it: The closer you store items to where you use them, the quicker and easier it is to clean up. For instance, if you knit at night while watching TV, create storage right near where you sit. It can be a decorative basket that slides under a coffee or end table. Whenever you put away your knitting, it goes into its basket and is stored immediately—instead of sitting it on the coffee table waiting to be returned to its home.

"Lid-off" policy: When and wherever possible, remove lids and doors. It means one less step to putting things back where they belong!

- "My rate is $65 an hour, but most of my clients opt for one of my packages, which are discounted. This often helps them commit to the process."

If you sense clients hesitating about your proposal, don't feel compelled to jump in. Let them think things through and make the commitment by themselves. Make yourself busy—dig into your bag and pull out your calendar, ready to schedule that first appointment. Most clients will sign on the spot; you can then move forward to setting the work schedule. If they tell you they need more time to decide or need to check with a spouse, I offer them my congratulations for having the courage to start this process and reassure them that whenever they are ready, they can just call to set up a first visit. Leave them with their assessment form, a business card, and words of inspiration and encouragement.

During the decision-making process, clients may ask what your guarantees are. The answer to this question is very delicate. You want to assure clients that you have what it takes to get the job done, but you also want them to realize that they, too, have a responsibility in the process. If clients are getting organized because of pressure from a boss, family member, or friend, they are more likely to ask this question. Be wary of such folks. If they take too much convincing, they may not be ready yet. I have never told clients I would refund their money if they weren't satisfied; what I have said is that I guarantee they will be satisfied with the work we do. Since I am always checking in with clients as we work, I have never needed to refund any money—nor has anyone ever told me they were dissatisfied.

Setting the Schedule

So clients have committed to your services and are excited to get started. Congratulations! Now pull out your calendar and look at dates. Schedule your first appointment and possibly standing appointments, if clients are willing. Remember, the more consistent you are with your appointments, the more progress you can make. Every Tuesday, every other Tuesday, whatever—just try to get a routine going for you and the clients. It helps you manage your schedule and keeps them on target.

After picking a date or dates, talk about the upcoming appointment. Review with them your "not calling to confirm" policy. I'm strict about this: Once we have an appointment on the calendar, I *do not* call to confirm. Here's why. In the beginning, when clients are faced with organizing their space or paperwork, the process can seem daunting until they meet with some success and gain momentum. If I call to confirm a day or two before an appointment, sometimes clients come up with excuses not to get together. If I leave it up to clients to cancel, however, I have fewer cancellations. For some reason, if you give clients wiggle room around their appointment, they may take it.

I make it very clear that I will show up on the designated date and time unless they hear from me otherwise, and that I expect they will be there. If for some reason they cannot make it, I explain to them that I need forty-eight hours' notice; otherwise I must charge them 50 percent of the scheduled visit fee. For instance, if we were scheduled for four hours, I'd bill them for two.

I have never had an issue with my cancellation or no-confirmation-call policy. Clients are aware that they need to be accountable, and as long as you are clear up front and include your policies in the Working Agreement you leave them with, you have done your part.

Creating a Plan for Your Clients

Your assessment visit with clients will let you know which spaces they feel the most stressed by. As you come up with your individual scheduling plan, then, you'll typically begin with one of those spaces. I say *typically* because clients will often discover new priorities between your initial visit and your first work session. They may now wish to start in the kitchen instead of the basement. Be flexible. As long as the switch does not hinder your overall work schedule and you are prepared, accommodate clients as best as you can. The trick is to have a plan, but go in with an open mind.

When it comes to organizing, you must stay flexible and keep your eyes and ears open at all times. You may know a great way to organize a particular space—you may even have picked out containers in your mind—but be wary of having it all figured out. The process of organizing is very mysterious at times.

There's nothing more mysterious, however, than clients. Their mess you can handle, bins and baskets sure, but what about their ever-changing emotional state? Let's turn to the ups and downs, the highs and lows of dealing with humans and their stuff.

The First Working Session

The first visit back with a client after he or she has signed up is as critical as the assessment visit. This is when the client will either be "happy" he signed on for a package or decide that he will pay you for today only and never call you back. It's your time to show 'em what you got! Some things to remember: Be timely, arrive five to ten minutes prior to session time, explain that you arrive early to get settled so you can start working on time. In the first minutes of the session review the plan for the day—an overview, not details—but give them an idea of what will happen in this first session. Pay close attention to the time as you go, giving yourself at least thirty to forty-five minutes to clean up and review what has been accomplished with the client.

At this first visit you really want some clear visible results. Truly, in every visit you want that; however, for this first visit it's highly recommended you get the client to feel a sense of relief and comfort in knowing he's made the right decision to hire you. Visible results can be a clear counter, an empty cabinet, or more structured cabinet. It can be boxes labeled with contents that were previously strewn across a room, but are now contained and identified.

Talk about any and all accomplishments that were made, whether they were physical or a mental change. For example, a client might have realized he doesn't need those trophies any more and will discard them before next visit, or he might have decided that keeping every edition of a magazine is not needed. Honor these changes in thought; it is very powerful for the client to hear. Now is when you pull out your homework list and include anything and everything to keep the client moving forward.

The Human Component

You will be working with clients one-on-one most of the time. As in any profession, you will encounter many different personality types; as an organizer, though, you'll be touching their stuff. Learning ways to handle a variety of situations will be helpful. If you come from a background that included lots of one-on-one work, get ready to use those skills. If you have never worked with individuals on such a personal or close basis, here are some basics to get you started.

Dealing with Emotions

Say you are going through a pile of papers, and the client comes across a death certificate for her mother who passed several months ago. The emotions she may express can sometimes be unsettling for you. What you need to remember is that it's okay for her to have these emotions, and it's up to you to know how to handle them. You can ignore them, which I don't recommend; you can acknowledge them and begin therapy sessions right there, another reaction I don't recommend; or you can say something as simple as, "I can see you've come across something that has stirred some emotions. If you'd like we can take a break, maybe get some water, and start again in a few minutes." This comment tells the client that she can share if she'd like, or she can get up and leave the room as a way to deal with her emotions, or she can reply, "No, I'm okay, let's continue." You've put her at ease by acknowledging that she's run into something emotional without making her feel she's being judged or asked to share her feelings. At the end of the visit or a short while after an emotional situation like this, you can remind the client that organizing can be an emotional process; you're happy to be assisting her and commend her for choosing to go on this journey. Explain that whatever emotions come up—during sessions or between them—are normal. All she has to do is breathe and know that she's on the right path: Working through the clutter is the first step in addressing the chaos she's feeling in her space and possibly her life.

There are times when you'll find that clients are resisting the organizing process, even though they're the ones who called you for help in the first place. They begin to get angry and aren't sure what to do with that anger. Some clients have avoided this process for years; now they are face-to-face with it. If you take it personally, it will only get worse. Understanding that anger typically masks other emotions, fear or sadness in particular, will help you better understand what clients may be going through. Make sure you are there serving them. They may need someone to push up against with their frustrations for a minute or two; if you don't react defensively, you might just be able to help them through this rough patch.

Why do clients get angry? Here are some of the deeper reasons that might be underlying their frustration:

- Someone is in their space, going through their stuff, and holding them accountable for it.
- They're realizing that they have let their lives get out of control.
- They'd rather be spending their time working, playing, you name it, than sorting and organizing.
- They're overwhelmed with the volume of stuff they have.

You handle angry clients much as you would deal with unexpected sadness: Acknowledge their feelings, then give options as to how to handle them.

You might say, "I can sense you're feeling some frustration. Maybe we can take a break for a few minutes, get something to drink, and start back in a little bit." I recommend that you make some adjustments when the clients are gone; if you can, switch to some other part of the organizing task for a while. For instance, if you are working on organizing papers and the sort is getting too tedious, maybe you can move some of the larger archive files to the basement or storage area for a change of pace. Changing the focus of the job, however briefly, can sometimes shift the energy in the room. It is important to know that each client is different; feel them out for the best ways to support them through the situation.

I did have a client once who became verbally abusive. It was a bit unnerving. I wasn't sure how to handle the situation, but I knew that I had to acknowledge her behavior and let her know it was inappropriate. I reminded myself not to take it personally—not easy, because she was beginning to blame me for our slow pace. My first thought was to defend myself and lash right back at her, but I stopped myself and responded: "I hear what you are saying and realize you are frustrated with how slow the process is moving. I can tell you that you are making good progress, and that what you are feeling is normal. I can't have you speaking to me the way you are right now. If you think we need to end our session for today, we can do that, but I think you're doing good work. Maybe just a short break will help." She walked out of the room without reacting, then came back in a few minutes with a glass of water and an apology. Shortly after that she was in tears: "I knew you said it would be tough at times, but I guess I didn't realize how tough." By not taking the client's anger personally, I was able to support her in a nonjudgmental way. This is what being a professional is all about.

While many organizers come from nursing, psychology, and other "caring" professions, it's not essential to have this background. It does help if you've dealt with people on a personal level before, but you can educate yourself as you go. I have included in "Recommended Reading" (appendix B) some books that I found especially helpful for understanding the human psyche. It is not our job to play therapist, but in the process of digging through stuff, many emotions do surface. We are our clients' support system whenever outbreaks occur; being able to professionally and humanely handle them is another feather in our cap.

Sofa Psychology

With the variety of organizing shows on cable television, you can be witness to the variety of emotions clients may go through during organizing. This is great training ground if you haven't had opportunities to work with clients one-on-one before. Don't forget the magic of television when seeing results so quickly and dramatically; it doesn't happen like that in the real world. As far as the anger, frustration, sadness, and blaming goes, you can learn a lot from these "real life" situations.

What's Your Organizing Personality?

When it comes to identifying different "organizing personalities"—the reasons why people end up surrounded by clutter and chaos in the first place—there are many books out there on the subject. I recommend that you learn as you go. If you start to label people, for instance, as pack rats or hoarders, you are likely to treat them differently than you would individuals just who need help with organization. Yes, all people have reasons for clutter, and yes, it will be important for you to assist them in identifying what got them to where they are now. Still, labeling them, even wholly for your own purposes, serves no one. *Leave the labeling and therapy for someone else.*

There are people who keep everything, have a hard time throwing things away. There are those who need to have everything out in plain view—or just the opposite, who need to have everything out of sight, even if it's chaos behind the scenes. Some folks can't be bothered to put things away, while others want a place for everything, but can't seem to create those places. Whatever the case, you can usually identify the issues during your first visit and will begin to get a sense of what type of organizing support clients will need. The more clients you work with, the better you'll become at adapting your 4-Step formula to each individual.

This is the advantage of using the formula: It works for all personality types. It is your job as the professional to create a plan of action that is appropriate for the situation. Big job? You may need assistance in the form of extra hands. I don't recommend bringing in extra hands in the beginning of your work with clients, as it might get unruly. Having a way to refer this client to another, more seasoned organizer who can help out on the project or mentor you, may be a great way to learn how to manage a bigger project and make a great business connection at the same time.

I've had clients announce to me that they were hoarders or pack rats—or worse, tell me they're just lazy. I respond, "Thanks for the warning, but I don't believe in creating labels, I believe in creating solutions. We all live our lives differently. I'd like to help you create an environment that supports who you are and what's important to you. So let's get started."

Finding the Clients

You've set your business up, you have a name you love, you have forms ready to go, you're excited about organizing your first closet, or kitchen, or paperwork mess—and now it's just a matter of finding the clients! Where are all the messy, disorganized people? Is there a particular place to go to find them? Once you find them, how do you get them to take action?

Most individuals have never thought about working with a professional organizer to help them create systems or eliminate their clutter or chaos. They see it as their own private battle. Maybe they feel that if they had the time, or if they weren't so lazy, they could take care of it themselves. Many don't know where to start, or they've made so many attempts at it before with no success, they feel it's useless and believe they're doomed to live in chaos forever. So we have to get them to notice us and pick up the phone.

Maybe they'll see your ad in their church bulletin, or a friend will tell them about you. Perhaps they'll read an article about or written by you, or they'll hear a radio interview that will inspire them to call you. Anytime you get your name and contact information in a person's line of sight, you've got a potential client. So get noticed! The next few pages will give you the opportunity to review many different methods of marketing and advertising. At the end of the chapter, you will have an opportunity to create a formal marketing plan.

There's really no science to it. You can read books and theories about marketing strategies, advertising venues, publicity pranks, you name it, but in the end your goal is to get noticed at the right time and by the right people, and to inspire them to call you to talk about how you can help them. It's up to you to determine what methods work best for you, your type of organizing, and the kinds of clients you are looking for.

There's one thing you should keep in mind as you begin this process: You don't want just any clients. You want the right clients. Soon after I launched my business, I was complaining that the phone wasn't ringing, and a good friend said to me, "The clients will come when they are ready, and you don't want them until they are." Of course, I wanted to argue that point and said, "I'll take any clients, whether they're ready or not!" But her advice was sound. When clients are ready, it makes the whole process smoother. When they're not...look out, that's a recipe for disaster.

There is little worse than clients who've been told to "get organized" and been pressured to call an organizer. This is the major reason why I have never offered gift certificates, and I recommend that you don't, either. Yes, I have had spouses call and say, "My husband really needs your help. I saw your ad and I want to buy him a gift certificate." But think about this: How would you like to receive a gift certificate for a face-lift? Or for a new weight loss diet? How would that feel? Imagine signing up a client brought to you kicking and screaming. Doesn't sound like a fun project, does it?

So with my friend's wise words in my ear, I enlisted my patience and created my first affirmation: *Clients come to me when they are ready, and I serve them in excellence.*

This felt good, but what to do in the meantime? I went back to getting noticed. How was I supposed to go about doing this on a shoestring budget? At first I spent too much time worrying about planning and not enough time doing—designing and redesigning the perfect brochure after plowing through countless marketing books to find the perfect solution. Then a friend called and asked if I would like to do a presentation on organizing for her mothers' group. She said they had only a small budget, but could pay me $100. I think I answered yes before she even finished the sentence. I was thinking about the money, knowing it would pay a bill or two for the business; I never anticipated what happened next.

The day came and I spoke for an hour about what I knew and loved, organizing. My title? "Organizing for the Health of It." I talked about messy kitchens, abominable bedrooms, paperwork landslides, and how we try to hide them, make excuses for them, argue about them, climb over them, and more. People laughed and enjoyed themselves. Then, to my utter delight, that night I booked another speaking gig and I scheduled an initial assessment with one of the moms! It was true: When the client was ready, all I had to do was make sure she knew how to find me and she'd call. How powerful and easy this was. That's the kind of marketing I like. That's the kind of marketing that works.

As you read the next few pages reviewing many methods of marketing and advertising, keep in mind your budget, your likes and dislikes, your target clients, and the time you have available.

Gift Certificate Etiquette

A great way to give the gift of organizing is a gift certificate from Wellness Possibilities. It's ingenious; you give one gift certificate and the recipient can use it for any service provider in the network. Just make sure you're a part of their local network! Visit www.wellnesspossibilities.com for more information. I founded this business with a friend to make finding resources easier, and I highly recommend you sign up. Use the code "DawnHowTo6" and get six months free with a six-month listing. I also use this gift certificate as a 'thank you' to my referral sources and clients. Since they can use it for more than organizing (e.g. to get a massage, take a yoga class, hire a personal trainer), it's a nice alternative to 'stuff' which we as organizers know most people have too much of already!

Marketing Assets

Before we get into the specific ways to get you and your business noticed, I'd like to talk about the most beneficial assets you have at your disposal. They are:

- **You:** Your talents, your passion, your drive to succeed. You will be available to lick stamps, write articles, speak publicly, design ads, and be creative. You may not necessarily be good at or enjoy doing all these things, but remember, you are your best advocate—and in the professional organizing business, you are the product as well.
- **The Internet:** Nowadays the Internet may be the only form of advertising some businesses use, leaving the paper world behind. Web ads, websites, search engines, social websites, blogging, even tweeting are all very powerful tools to get you noticed. Even social clubs and groups communicate on "loops" and can spread the word. If you're not savvy when it comes to the

Net, don't worry, you'll learn as you go. If you don't, there's always the next most powerful tool you have, and that's . . .

- **Your marketing team:** Family, friends, colleagues, business associates—these are all people available to assist you in your marketing efforts. Some will need to be compensated through commissions or in other ways, and some will not. This group can provide you with referrals and advertise your company through word of mouth. Keep these people in mind as you begin the marketing process. Last, but certainly not least, is . . .
- **Your budget:** Your budget will have a dramatic impact on your marketing efforts. As you will see in the next pages, ways to get noticed range in price from free to obscenely expensive. Determining your budget and working within it shouldn't be difficult, thanks to the many options available to you, but you'll still need to pay close attention to it.

With these thoughts in mind, let's take a look at the many methods of getting you and your business noticed.

Advertising

Creating an effective ad and finding the right place to list it is an art form. You want to get value for your dollars, of course, and advertising is a bit tricky in this regard. You never really know the readership of a particular magazine, place mat, or other periodical. It's about budget and trusting your gut at first. Once you have placed a few ads and have gotten responses (or not), you can begin to weed out some of these options.

Diner Place Mat Ads

I always check out the ads on these things, and I imagine many other people do, too. Besides, what else do you do when you're waiting for your food to come? You'd be surprised at what decisions are made over a cup of coffee. If you don't live in an area where diners are common, I'm sure there's a coffee shop or other family restaurant near you that prints ads on its menus. These ads could be costly, but they cover the local area and give you exposure. Most often people use their business card for this type of ad. My suggestion is to be a bit more creative and design something that lists all your essential information—just with a bit more flair.

Newsletters

Most local clubs and groups have newsletters. Mothers clubs' and Junior Leagues, for instance, send out newsletters periodically through the year. Even if you haven't spoken for them at a meeting, they are sometimes looking for advertisers to help defray the costs of newsletter printing. Most would be happy to include you, especially if your service is of interest to their particular group. The rates are typically very reasonable. When you speak to your contact person from such a group, it's also a good time to ask if they need someone to present at a monthly meeting! You may even be able to trade a presentation to their group for an ad or two in their newsletter.

Having been a part of some of these groups myself, I can tell you that this is a powerful advertising source. Members talk and share experiences and resources. Remember, the experience of organizing is a very personal one; people want to know they are working with someone who is trustworthy.

Newspapers and Magazines

Local newspapers and magazines are good opportunities to generate local interest for your business; however, newspapers are a less attractive option. They don't hang around long in the home so your ad will be in front of someone only for a short period of time. Local or regional magazines, however, are kept for much longer and, while the cost may be a bit higher than newspaper, you'll get more mileage out of it. Find a magazine targeted to a special niche market or type of client. To start, I used regional magazines that covered several counties. They highlighted local services and were geared towards moms and families.

Typically, the more times you commit to advertising in a year, the better the rate you will receive. Repetition, they say, is helpful. I would tend to agree; I committed to one local magazine for an entire year to get the best rate. I calculated that if I got two clients, each of whom I could bill for fifteen or more hours, then the year would be paid for...and I did.

Phone Book Ads or Listings

It's nice exposure to be in the phone book, but the expense may be prohibitive. First, you must have a business phone line, not a residential line; as I discussed in chapter 2, this is considerably more expensive. Second, you must commit to the listing or display ad for one year, since phone books are printed only annually. If you are interested in something more than just a simple line listing—a display ad, for instance—your cost goes up considerably. Prices vary widely from book to book; also note that some now have a presence on the web. My suggestion for your first year in business is that your advertising dollars are better spent elsewhere. Once you have established yourself, review your budget and reconsider this method.

If, however, you opted for a business phone line from the start, odds are that you got information about what type of listing is automatically included and what your options are to upgrade it. If not, take care of this now: Find out the best phone book in your area, request rates, and see how they compare with other advertising venues.

Place of Worship Bulletin and Calendar Ads

Many people, when in church waiting for the services to begin, like to have a look-see at who is advertising in the church bulletins. I certainly do. If there is a particular service I am looking for, or interested in, choosing to work with someone listed in the church bulletin makes me feel as if I'm supporting my community. These ads vary in price depending on the area they cover. For instance, you may place one ad that will be featured in numerous churches throughout your community. I found these to be a bit pricey, but still worth some thought.

Resource Directories

There are resource guides for a variety of services similar to yours. For instance, there is a holistic practitioner's guide that lists all types of practitioners in my area. This would be another way to target your advertising at the local community. If you can find resource guides like this in your area, see if they have a section for organizing; if not, see if they'll start one. Or maybe you specialize in dealing with a particular type of client and can be listed in a resource under that heading. For example, one nearby hospital has a directory that lists resources for ADD/ADHD clients. If this is a market you are interested in pursuing, try placing an ad there.

Television and Radio Commercials

While this is very costly, it can also be a very powerful way to get noticed. Cable television in your local area is a good place to start. Ask questions about fees and what it takes to get a commercial made. You may be directed to a local college that has an advertising program; students looking for projects might do yours for free or at a very reduced rate. This is probably too expensive for a beginning organizer, but when you're ready and have the funds, it's worth doing.

Supermarkets

There are three new ways to advertise in the local supermarket. Not all supermarkets offer these options, but many do. First, there are television sets at the deli counter and now at the checkout counter. These run thirty- to sixty-second commercials that keep shoppers busy while their order is being processed. They are entertaining and eye-catching, but something must be missing because they don't seem to work very well. I know two individuals who posted ads on these TVs. It was very expensive, and after six months neither one had received a single call. I do think this is a great idea; it may just take time to catch on.

Shopping carts offer another advertising resource. The front and back of each cart feature panels for which you can buy advertising space. It's an interesting idea, and definitely a way to get exposure.

The third option is one I've seen in my local store, where a train attached to the ceiling circles the checkout area. Yes, you heard me, a train. It's a miniature, and each car is posted with a business card or ad for a local service or business. As you stand in line, you hear the train coming, look up, and see the information. I know it works because I can think of four businesses right off the bat that advertise on this train. They get noticed!

While not every grocery store has TV sets, or trains, the idea is to get in front of your potential clients and get noticed. Advertising in the grocery store certainly does that. Talk to your local supermarket about setting up creative advertising options.

Web Directories

As I mentioned earlier, www.wellnesspossibilities.com is a directory that I created out of need for a place to send clients to find additional resources to help along their journey. We have professional organizers in the directory along with other wellness professionals. This is considered a Wellness Directory. If you're looking for a directory specifically for organizers, then NAPO may be the place, or www.findmyorganizer .com is another. Also listing organizers is www.servicemagic.com. Being present on the web is very powerful, so when it comes to your advertising budget I would recommend putting Internet directories higher on your list than print ads. The other nice thing about these directories is that you typically don't design your ad, but rather, the listings are posted based on information you input. The directories are very quick and easy to get up and running.

Website Ads and Banners

Many website owners sell advertising space in the form of text or banner ads. These spaces may be free, or there may be a fee. If there is a fee, you want to make sure that the site you're considering gets considerable traffic. Your best bet is sites that support the work you do—closet installers, garage storage companies, interior decorators, Feng Shui consultants, or product companies. There are ways to find out how many "click-throughs" you get from these sites. Talk to your web hosting service or your computer help person to find out about this.

There are other ways to get listed or linked on websites, too. Most professional organizer associations have "Find an Organizer" pages where you can get listed. Of course, you need to be a member of the organization and/or pay a monthly fee. These fees are reasonable, and the people visiting the site are good prospects—they have already sought out information on organizing and are ready to get down to business.

You can also link with other websites. For example, there are services and businesses that I recommend to clients frequently. I have included their links on the resources page of my own website, and they have reciprocated with a link to mine. I have found these to be worthwhile relationships. Also, clients have reported to me that they've used not only businesses listed on my site, but also businesses linked on *those* sites. The power of the Internet and referrals is amazing!

Learn from Experience

Debbie Ennis, small-business owner
"Whenever I see a new advertising idea, before I invest a dime, I like to call others who are advertising in that way and see how it's working for them."

Ad Design

Whether you design your own ads, ask a friend, hire a professional, or get assistance from the publication you're working with, always keep it simple, clean, and uncluttered.

Your header should be eye-catching, white letters on a black background; the body of the ad should be the opposite, black on white. The most readable fonts are Helvetica, sans serifs, and Arial. Graphics, if any, should be simple and support your message.

Include the following information in the body of your text: your business name, phone number, web address, services (bulleted, if possible), and an offer or call to action. No matter how big your ad space is, don't add anything more than these details. Remember, most clients are looking for a service that can help them create calm, order, and serenity; your ad should exemplify that.

Including a particular drawing or picture in your ads can be helpful, especially if you're doing the designing yourself. I had a drawing created for me by a local artist; I purchased the rights to it and can use it in any and all advertising or marketing pieces.

I found another nifty illustration online in a clip art database. I can use it for free.

As you budget for advertising, don't forget to consider the cost of ad design in addition to fees for actually running ads. Most publications that sell ad space have graphic artists available to assist you in designing an ad. However, these media are in the business of selling space; they're not in the business of selling your business or service. This certainly doesn't mean they won't generate an ad that gets responses, but to truly sell your business, it must have your touch. Hiring a graphic artist that you have selected based on his or her style and the look you are interested in creating goes a long way toward creating ads you love and that represent you and your business. Images created by an independent graphic artist can also be used in any other publication or flyer.

Marketing

There are all kinds of ways to get your name and services out there in front of the public. I've listed many of them in the discussion that follows. These methods are mostly the tried-and-true traditional ones. Never stop thinking, however, about inventive new ways. Sometimes being creative and different is what will set you apart from the rest.

The biggest changes in marketing have been in networking. Traditionally this was done in person, maybe even a little via e-mail. But with the explosion of Internet networking sites (i.e., Facebook, Twitter, Linkedin, MySpace, Ning, and blogs), the use of the Internet can reach thousands of people instantly. Take a look at all of the following ideas for marketing and then decide where to focus your attention.

Articles

What a great way to craft a reputation as the expert in your field! There's just one caveat: Writing timely, informative articles can get you noticed in a hurry, so if you're new to the business, make sure you're ready for the exposure articles may get you before you start writing.

Articles Written *By* You

I have found that a great way to break into publishing is to write articles pertinent to either the time of year or a particular organizing topic. Around the holiday season, for example, you may want to submit "The Top 10 Time-Savers for the Holiday Season." Newspapers may choose to run this article and will hopefully include your business information with it. They sometimes use it in coordination with an article they already have in the works, or they may let your piece take the lead. Once reporters have you in their database as the expert organizer in the area, they may reach out to you for future articles. You will also get a lot of phone calls and website activity from these articles. You may be asked to speak on the topic, so if you're new, wait until you are ready for this type of exposure.

Another tip is to try submitting the same article to many different publications. The only time this becomes an issue is if someone offers to pay you for the article. Sounds great, right? Yes, but remember that receiving payment will restrict you from having it published elsewhere. One organizer I know suggests refusing this payment and in exchange asking the publication to print a more detailed contact information box with the article. For instance, instead of simply including your company name with an article, you can ask that in lieu of payment, the periodical print the following: "For more information on getting your papers in order, call Dawn at (555) 555-5555 or visit www.BalanceAndBeyond.com." If a publication wants exclusive rights to your article, however, this tactic won't work; then you'll need to decide if the fee alone is worthwhile.

National Happiness-Is-a-Warm-Organizer Day

Stuck for ideas on writing your first article? There are many organization-themed calendar days that may be of interest to publications:

January, entire month: Get Organized Month

January, second Monday: National Clean Off Your Desk Day

February, second Tuesday: Clear Out Your Computer Day

March, first full week: National Procrastination Week

March, second Tuesday: National Organize Your Home Office Day

March, last week: Clutter Awareness Week

April, third week: Organize Your Files Week

August, first week: Simplify Your Life Week

September, entire month: Self-Improvement Month

October, entire month: Clean Out Your Files Month

October, first full week: National Get Organized Week

Articles Written *About* You

Getting a reporter to write an article about you and/or your business is like finding the golden ticket in the Willy Wonka bar. The opportunity to generate clients is considerable. So how can you get reporters interested in writing about you and your work? One way is to do volunteer work with a local group or organization. It's a way of getting experience, meeting individuals in your community, and getting exposure. Suppose your community is scheduling a townwide yard sale and needs volunteers to get things organized. Well, this is perfect for you! Jump right in and assist. In exchange, ask the organizers if they are willing to mention your business in the advertising and literature: "Services generously donated by . . ." Not only will you be introduced to many local homeowners, but you'll get experience and exposure as well.

Another approach? Simply call your local papers and tell them you are a new business, and would be willing to work with them on creating an interest piece. You can even offer to do a free cubicle or office makeover for someone at the paper or for one of its readers. Offering to do actual work will provide reporters with before-and-after pictures to add to their article.

Press Releases

Press releases are a great tool to get you exposure in local papers, especially the kind that list all the local happenings. This is a great place to announce the start of your business, any workshops you might be holding, and other community events you organize. Send it to all the local papers, magazines, and anyone else you can think of.

It's up to the editor whether press releases get printed. Make yours more about the benefit to readers and the general public, and less about you and your business, for your best chance to see print. If it seems too much like an advertisement, it probably won't be run.

If a local club invites you to speak, ask whether they create press releases for their meetings. If not, offer to write one for them and submit it. It's great exposure for both you and the group. If they do write-up press releases, ask to see this one prior to release to make sure your contact information is all-inclusive. If you are offering a free-of-charge presentation, they are usually willing to accommodate you.

Be sure your press release covers the five W's of journalism: who, what, where, when, and why. See a sample on the facing page.

Press Release

FOR IMMEDIATE RELEASE: 9 am, EST, June 15, 2011
KILL DATE: July 28, 2011

Attention: Hometown Happenings Editor

Contact: Dawn Noble
Balance and Beyond
P.O. Box 131
Middletown, NJ 07772
Phone: (555) 555–5555
Fax: (555) 555–5556
E-mail: dawn@balanceandbeyond.com
Website: www.BalanceAndBeyond.com

Free **Workshop to Help the Small-Business Owner**

In celebration of Get Organized Month, one of New Jersey's top professional organizers will be conducting a *free* workshop designed to teach small-business owners specific techniques for setting up foolproof filing systems, eliminating piles of paper, and freeing up hours of time for other business priorities.

Dawn Noble, a professional organizer and home-based business owner herself, will provide other business owners with information that will eliminate excess paper and create reliable, simple filing systems.

The workshop is free and open to the public.
Thursday, July 28, 7:30–9:30 p.m.
Middletown Library, Monmouth Road, Middletown, NJ
To learn more details and to register, please visit www.balanceandbeyond.com
or call (555) 555–5555.

Brochures and Panel Cards

You know my thoughts about the brochure: It's a nice piece, but most individuals can't find it once they bring it home to their mess anyway. Instead I suggest using a single-panel card that lists the basics of what you do and how to contact you, directing people to your website for further information. I use these at presentations and meetings; I've occasionally left some with local coffee shops or other retailers that seemed to have good foot traffic. Panel cards cost about a third as much as brochures. If you do choose to print brochures, try focusing them for individuals who ask for more information, rather than just considering them handouts. See the next page for examples of these materials.

Business Cards

The business card is an indispensable tool to have with you at all times. I'm forever finding myself in conversations that begin, "What do you do for a living?"—and the topic of professional organizing is always a hot one. Everyone likes to share war stories of their personal mess. I make sure I always have a card ready to hand these folks.

I recommend using the back of your card as well as the front. Here are examples of some of the information you might want to include:

- A list of the services you offer
- A set of questions people can ask themselves to determine if they need an organizer
- An offer of some kind; for example, "Call today and mention how you found out about my services and receive 5 percent off initial assessment"

Keep your card's design simple, clean, and uncluttered. No fold-overs, weird shapes, or gimmicks. Keep it horizontal, not vertical, and please, get your cards professionally printed! I don't care how good your printer is, the business cards printed at home just can't compare to professionally printed ones. Even if your budget is tight, this is where you should spend the extra dollars. I cannot stress enough how important this is. You want your services to be considered top notch, so if the only representation of your business potential clients have is below par, then they will assume your business is, too.

Balance & Beyond

Information for better living

Tired of living a life of chaos?

Do your days run one into the other with little time for living?

Tired of the papers and piles on every horizontal surface?

Do you wish you could just catch up?

If so, read on...

We at Balance and Beyond are here to help individuals and families *turn chaos into order*. We can help you put your life back on track so you can start living life, instead of just surviving it!

Don't waste another minute dealing with the frustration of a disorganized, chaotic life.

Don't buy another book about organizing or time management... you don't have time to read it anyway!

Rely on us to provide you with everything you need to get your life in order without having to weed through the information that doesn't apply to you.

What types of information do we provide?

- Paperwork Control
- De-Cluttering
- Organizing
- Time Management
- Household Cleaning
- Family Fun & Management

How do we provide it?

- Private Consultation
- Group/Club Presentations
- Public Workshops

If you are ready to commit to a more organized, stress free life; ready to start living instead of just surviving... then call us. We are ready to help you get there!

Call and speak with Dawn to discuss your particular needs:

phone: 555-555-5555

Visit our website to check out our monthly contest & to see our workshop schedule!

www.BalanceAndBeyond.com

Coupon Packs

You'll see plenty of these during your organizing sessions with clients. Most people feel the need to open each one of these they get in the mail, even though they all typically contain coupons from the same advertisers. For some reason, they're convinced this one will have a bargain they just can't pass up. I have spoken to advertisers who use this venue; they tell me that the response has been great, even when their service was a pricey one. For instance, a roofing contractor told me that he gets a good percentage of his business from this type of advertising, so it's not just for small-ticket items. Check out Valpak (www.valpak.com) and Money Mailer (www.moneymailer.com).

Direct Mail Letters

Yes, I tried this. Yes, it costs quite a bit of money. No, it did not work for me. While this may be a worthwhile way of advertising for many ventures, odds are that with the budget you have and the fact that organizing is a very personal process for most people, direct mail to individuals is a tough route to go.

You will need to purchase a mailing list, which is fairly pricy. Add in the cost of the mailer itself as well as postage and you're looking at a pretty expensive option. It may work to announce workshops or local presentations, but the chances of having clients call you based on a letter they received in the mail is very slim. If all of this still hasn't scared you off and you're convinced that a direct mail piece might work, think about doing postcards first (more on postcards later).

Flyers

Creating flyers is simple if you're creative and adept at using templates on your computer. Make sure that your message is clear, that the flyer doesn't appear cluttered, and that your contact information is bold and easy to find.

There are all sorts of ways to use flyers.

Inserted into Newspapers

Print up your flyers on standard 8.5-by-11-inch paper, bring them to a newspaper company, and they'll charge you a fee—typically $75 to $125 per thousand—to insert your piece into their papers. This is a nice alternative to an ad, because it's more likely to get noticed. Be timely: Tie in your flyer with spring cleaning, New Year's resolutions, back-to-school preparation, whatever it might be. This is also a great way to announce a local workshop or promotion you have going on.

Posted

You can post your flyers in many different areas—with permission, of course: bulletin boards, windows, display boards, and more. Great locations include coffeehouses, supermarkets, and children's gyms or nursery schools (if this is a good target audience for you). Or you could try colleges, office buildings, and train stations. Be creative and keep an eye out for good places to post information targeted at your ideal type of client:

- Put them up at your local grocery store to offer spring cleaning and organizing services.
- Distribute them to retirement communities offering your help with paperwork.
- Post them with storage-space companies, focusing on all the ways you can help folks clean out their units.

Handouts

Okay, so this method isn't the greatest. It could be an effective option for creative souls, though. Have someone hand out flyers in a likely location. The third week of April is Clean Out Your Files Week, for instance, so you might hire someone to distribute flyers in front of an office building for two hours every morning as employees come to work, offering a discount for anyone who calls "this week" to schedule an appointment. Use your imagination; I bet you'll come up with lots of ideas.

Handouts or Freebies: Magnets, Pens, Pads

Be careful when it comes to tchotchkes. You are in the organizing field, and everything you say, do, and give out is a reflection of how you help others eliminate chaos in their life. If your handouts are useless or become dust collectors, you're only adding to the mess! Magnets are good, since most people put them right on the fridge and thus have your name in front of them pretty consistently. Pens and pads are also popular, useful items. Beyond these basics, though, think twice.

The cost of such giveaways can be reasonable, especially if you buy in bulk. They are great for presentations and workshops. You might also use them much as you would your business cards: If folks ask you for your card, hand them a pen as well!

Newsletters and e-Zines

Writing your own newsletter can be a great way to get people interested in getting organized or learning more about your business in general. Still, there are a couple of questions you'll want to consider first: How much time will it take to create a good newsletter, and who will you send it to?

Unfortunately, newsletter costs can be prohibitive. A couple of less expensive options are printing up a simple black-and-white newsletter on a single sheet of paper, and creating an e-zine.

My suggestion? Pull out some favorite newsletters or e-zines that you've received and ask yourself what you like about them. Try to duplicate these features. Remember to keep your newsletters timely, simple, fun, and informative. Too much advertising will turn readers off.

Think about including some of the following in your newsletter:

- Customer profiles with before-and-after pictures
- Information on organizing products
- A "tip of the week/month" column, especially if your business focuses on a particular niche area in organizing
- A computer support section
- Website recommendations

Your newsletter doesn't have to be monthly; it can be quarterly, or bimonthly, or whatever you choose. Keep its design consistent. If you send it out in envelopes, be sure the envelopes you choose reflect your design in color and/or logo. If you send a self-mailer—a folded piece of paper that needs no envelope—keep the look the same outside and in.

Be sure to send your newsletter—whether by regular mail or e-mail—only to those who have given you permission. Anytime you speak at a public event, bring along a sign-up form that includes the question of whether attendees would like to be included on your mailing list. I've found that if I state right there on the permission form that I only send out quarterly newsletters, more people sign up. The same goes for your website—have a spot where visitors can opt in for your newsletter.

Creating a newsletter may be too daunting a prospect if you're just start out in business. Still, it's a good option to keep in mind as a second- or third-phase marketing method.

Postcards

Postcards are a less expensive marketing method than direct mail letters: Postage is cheaper, and you don't need envelopes. I recommend sending these only to current or past customers. You can use them as seasonal reminders of your cleanup and maintenance services; they're also a good way to advertise your availability to host a workshop. You can even leave a stack of postcards behind after any presentations you give.

The nice thing about postcards is that you can catch folks' attention as they skim through their mail. The front of your card should be a great image of some kind—perhaps before-and-after pictures—something potential clients will want to hold on to for inspiration until they're ready to call you.

Postcards can also be designed to be used as handouts and not as mailers. Ranging in size from 3 x 5 up to 5 x 7 inches or larger, they can carry more information than a business card but not as much as the panel card or brochure. They are very cost effective. Some good resources are available online, just search on "postcard printing" and you'll find many. Do your research, ask around, and compare pricing; it varies wildly from one supplier to another.

Networking

Of all the marketing methods out there, networking is my very favorite; I can't speak highly enough about this powerful tool. Now, it *will* require you to get out in front of people, usually strangers, and speak comfortably about your business. If this scares the pants off you, then you'll have to do some preparation work, or else budget in a marketing person to network for you. If this sounds like more than you're ready for, it needn't be—it can be an informal arrangement in which you enlist the support of a good friend or acquaintance, then work out commission payments for any business he or she secures. Either way—whether you're out there networking or someone's doing it on your behalf—this is a very powerful and inexpensive way to build your career.

Association and Trade Shows

All kinds of associations hold trade shows throughout the year—exhibitions in which individual businesses set up booths explaining their products and services.

Many make excellent venues for organizers, because you can meet prospective clients face-to-face. It can be a costly venture, of course: You'll need to have a booth of some sort and handouts such as a postcard or panel card. Still, trade shows are often a great way to get to know other business owners, talk to prospects, and get exposure.

If you'd like to jump into this arena, start by learning more about the particular show you're considering. How many people does the association anticipate at their show? How many years have they been doing this? How are they planning to advertise the event? Are there other services like yours attending? How many vendors are there? What are the show's hours? How far do you need to travel with your booth and materials and how early do you have to be there to get set up? The answers to these questions will give you a better idea of whether the show is worth your time, and if you'll need help in setting things up.

Think carefully about whether the show's theme is appropriate for you. I once exhibited at a wedding trade show in a mall, one featuring anything to do with getting married. I thought, *Who wouldn't want to get organized before getting married? All that stuff each person owns...wouldn't it be nice to get it organized before melding it together?* I couldn't have been more wrong! I sat between DJs and florists, limousine services and caterers. No one was interested in getting organized, just planning their weddings. It was a very long couple of days.

Trade Show Tips

- Bring a friend—someone who knows your services and can staff the booth when you need a break.

- Bring your "Favorite Tips Sheet" to hand out along with any clutter quiz or other simple one sheets that have your business info on them and are fun and inspiring.

- Some shows include workshops and presentations; find out if you can host one.

- Don't forget to wear comfortable shoes!

I have attended a wide range of trade shows and seen a variety of booth designs. The booth that works best for me—the one that generates the most conversation and new contacts—is what I call my before booth. In it I re-create a typical "before" scene—what a space looks like before a professional organizer gets there and works magic. I make sure to have my portfolio of afters to show visitors, too!

Any number of trade show attendees approach my before booth with comments such as, "Oh my gosh, my kitchen table looks just like that," or "Did you actually *see* my dining room?" This starts up the conversation with a good laugh. I then have the opportunity to talk about my services and everything I have to offer. There's no need for hard sell; everyone gets exactly what it is I can do for them, and they remember our conversation because it started with a laugh. When they're ready, they will call.

Business Networking Groups

Business networking can be one of the most cost-effective ways to introduce you and your business to potential clients. There are community and professional organizations as well as trade associations. These groups meet weekly, monthly, and bimonthly to help members support one another in growing their businesses, especially via referrals. Meetings can also be terrific places to practice your 15- to 30-second business commercial. Remember, these groups can be both local and national, which can be a real advantage later on if you are interested in growing your speaking business.

Don't make the mistake of joining too many groups. Try attending several meetings to determine which group or groups are appropriate for your type of organizing before you join. Then put together a top five list and work your way down, maybe joining two or three depending on your schedule.

Here are some of the groups you might want to check out:

- Business Networking International (BNI; www.bni.org)
- Chamber of Commerce (www.uschamber.com)
- Small-business associations (local chapters)
- National Association of Professional Organizers (NAPO; www.napo.net)

This is just a partial listing; look in your area to find the right one for you. Ask local and home-based business owners, if you know any, which groups they have been involved in and what their thoughts are.

The Internet

One of the biggest marketing explosions in recent history is the advent of the Internet. Using the Internet and social networking sites can be as easy or as complicated and involved as you want to make it. To start, ask yourself: How much time do you want to dedicate to this particular method of networking? Second, what is your knowledge base of one or all of these sites? Is this something you will be doing on your own?

If there is one you're familiar with, like Facebook, I would start there. Take some educational courses on using Facebook to build your business (there are plenty out there). Or pick up a book on Internet usage to give you the nuts and bolts. See if this is something you're willing to invest time into.

Next, pick one other social site and research the same thing (how it works, what's involved, recommended steps to take to make it work to build your business, etc.). Each of these venues has different pros and cons. Then ask yourself the first questions again: time, commitment, knowledge of the process, and what it will take. This all goes a long way to creating something successful in any one of these particular venues.

For example, I started a group page for one of my businesses on Facebook and quickly fell off maintaining it regularly. Soon I pulled it down because the out-of-date page was doing more harm than good. You don't want information to be stale

Facing Facebook

"You would be amazed at how marketing and having a business profile on Facebook has changed the face of marketing world-wide. Facebook has practically surpassed Google as a search engine; there are more than 500 million active users and many small businesses now have a presence on Facebook! I am passionate about making sure you have all the puzzle pieces in place for a strong foundation for growing your business effectively on Facebook." says Louise Crooks of Keysto-Clarity Coaching, www.keystoclarity.com. She specializes in working with soul-o-preneurs looking to maximize their Facebook presence, find their ideal clients, and market their expertise inexpensively and effectively.

or appear old, so knowing what you are willing to do and how often you can update a site will help.

I next tried blogging. I started with just learning about what it took to be a blogger. Then I did it for a summer personally for family and friends, learning how to post pictures, links, websites, etc. I had about a six- to eight-week learning curve for me to learn the process. Unfortunately, the moment I stopped doing it, I seemed to loose all the steps I needed to do it easily. Every time I sat to blog, it felt like climbing a small hill. Not horrible, but certainly not easy for me.

I recommend extensively investigating any of these areas that you'd like to use, try it out personally first, and then, when you feel like you have it mastered and it's something you can maintain, develop your business blog, Facebook page, group, or whatever.

Public Relations Person

Wouldn't it be nice to hire a person to get you noticed? You can. PR professionals are experienced at their craft and have connections in many different areas of publicity. Do your research and by all means get references for anyone you're thinking of working with. Then interview several professionals, discussing what it is they will do for you, how they measure success, and their contract and payment requirements.

When you're just starting out, hiring a PR person may be overkill—but it is something to keep in mind. Once you are ready to embark upon a speaking career or are ready to grow your business and need more exposure, having your own PR professional can be invaluable.

Referrals

Referrals will be one of your strongest marketing tools, and interestingly enough, all you have to do is what you do best! After I spoke at a local church meeting, a woman in the audience immediately went home and called her sister. "Dawn's exactly who you've been looking for," the woman said. "She can help with your stuff." In turn, the sister called me the very next day, and I began working with her a week later.

That's not all. Once she'd worked with me, she again spoke to her sister—the one who'd attended my presentation. "You *have* to hire Dawn yourself. You met her and liked her, and I've worked with her and I know she can help you." I started working with that sister the week after that. It was a referral free-for-all! It is a good idea to keep a record of referrals. (See the Referral Record Log on page 217 to get started.

Did I say free? Yes, most referrals are free, brought to you by someone who's had a good experience with you or knows of you and your services and recommends you to someone else. And what do you say to this person for doing this? Yes, that's right, you say "thank you." Thank-yous are a critical part of the referral process. They can come in the form of a handwritten note, a plant, even a fruit basket; what matters is that you do it.

> Janet,
>
> Thank you for sharing your organizing adventure with your friend Ellen. She was so inspired by your hard work and success with your home office that she is considering tackling her own organizing projects.

You might want to set up a formal system for referral thank-yous. For instance, you can print on your business card or tell your clients and contacts that for every person they refer who signs up for services, they get an hour's consultation free, or they receive your *101 Ways to Get Through the Holidays* booklet, or they receive a commission. Acknowledging their efforts in some way will give them incentive to continue spreading the word. If you're uncomfortable with these formal arrangements, it's fine to send your thanks in more traditional formats.

Clients beget Clients

This might be the perfect time to send your past clients a "reminder" postcard in time for the holiday or other organizing season. The clients inevitably talk about their experiences and may even recommend that others work with you, so give them the reason to do so!

Social Clubs

Whether mothers' clubs, parent–teacher groups, or the Junior League, small social clubs offer another powerful networking opportunity. If you know any members, ask if they might post a flyer for you, or place your business cards at a meeting. If they're former clients, see if they'll share their experiences with their group. If you're ready, you can even offer to speak at a meeting. These clubs are often in need of speakers, and the topic of organizing is a hot one. Find an area of organizing you can talk about comfortably and create a short presentation. Offer this free of charge or at a reasonable fee. If you're speaking for free, you can request a mailing list of their members or ad space in their next newsletter in exchange.

Even though these groups may be small in size, their reach is broad. A member of one social club may also belong to another and mention you and your services there. I got a lead into the corporate world from one of these small-group presentations. A member of a social club I spoke to was in the human resource department of a Fortune 500 company. About five or six months after she heard my presentation, she contacted me and signed me up to make a presentation before more than a hundred of the executives at her company—at a very nice corporate rate. Of course, it was just the chance I was looking for to expand my business horizons.

I've had clients call up to two years after seeing me present to schedule an appointment. The fact that they held on to my card for that long was impressive; the fact that they could find it in all their chaos was amazing! I've also had clients schedule an assessment visit with me immediately after the presentation. This was my main source of growth during my first two years in business.

Speaking

Speaking in front of a group of people is number one on the list of things feared by the general public—according to *The Book of Lists,* it even outranks that of dying. If this is something you've been avoiding, you may want to do some practicing or get some coaching before taking on a speaking engagement. If you've done this before in another line of business, however, then it's a skill you should definitely exploit.

Strategic Alliances

Try setting up a formal referral agreement with other businesses. Known as strategic alliances, these agreements include a referral fee (the industry standard is typically 10 percent) and other advantages. Consider setting up such relationships with moving companies, real estate agencies, accountants, storage facilities, closet installers, Feng Shui consultants, interior decorators—indeed, any professionals who deal directly with homeowners or actually go into the home.

TV and Radio Interviews

Landing a television or radio interview can be very powerful and typically costs you nothing other than a trip to the salon and a new outfit. Kidding aside, if you get a call to do either a television or radio interview, it might be a good idea to speak with a coach or at least practice with someone you know. The coaching may be well worth it, helping both your confidence and your presentation. Try asking your interviewer ahead of time what questions will be asked; this can go a long way toward helping you prepare for this great opportunity.

The media is always looking for interesting stories or information. Contact any relevant television or radio station to discuss how an interview might interest them. A particular client and/or story may be appealing. Of course, you must always get clients' approval before offering up their stories; although you can use fictitious names, reporters are typically more interested in the real people.

I once had a client whose parents were about to be evicted because their apartment was considered unsafe. They had two weeks to get the space up to code before the final inspection. The daughter called me in and her parents and I went to work immediately, tackling years' worth of possessions stuffed into a one-bedroom apartment. We found interesting homes for some of their cherished items: The local museum was interested in her father's camera collection, which dated back to the 1920s. We donated several large pieces of furniture to the local library, including a library table itself. We sold several book collections on eBay; an auction house was interested in purchasing several paintings.

I told the story to a reporter, mentioning where some of the stuff had gone, and he liked the idea of following all these pieces to their new homes. The museum and library loved the publicity as well. My client's mother and father were interviewed and shared their experiences. Best of all, in the end they didn't have to leave their apartment, and they found good homes for family heirlooms.

Workshops and Seminars

If you're new to the business, you may want to wait awhile before presenting a seminar or workshop; it helps to have some experiences under your belt to talk about. Still, if you're comfortable speaking in public and knowledgeable about a special area of organizing, it can be an excellent marketing opportunity. For instance, if your background is in health care and you know a lot about insurance forms and such, offer to give workshops to the residents of nearby senior housing or assisted living facilities. The word of your talents will spread, and other groups may be interested.

Hosting your own workshop—in particular filling the room—may be more difficult than you think. When I first started my business, I had some solid experience behind me in teaching workshops for my previous employer; I figured it'd be simple to hold my own. What a reality check! After I had booked about ten different dates at a local hotel—and canceled them all when no one signed up—I realized I just wasn't well enough known yet to fill a room. I do teach workshops and seminars quite often these days, but always in conjunction with a group or corporation that hires me; it's up to these folks to find the participants.

Another way to fill a room is to teach at a local adult and continuing education school. They advertise your workshop or class information in their flyers or booklets that go out to all the local homeowners. Although the fees you collect are lower than if you held a workshop on your own, because the school takes a percentage, your exposure in the community is greater.

Creating Your Own Marketing Plan

You already created your business plan, back in chapter 1; now it's time to create your marketing plan. In my opinion, a marketing plan is by far the more important of the two documents at this stage. Yes, your business plan will become critical if and when you attempt to find financial backing. Your marketing plan, however, is designed to keep you on task and on budget as you grow your business. It defines your target audience, identifies your services, and describes how you will generate clients. Marketing will take up a lot of your time and budget in the early stages of your business, and it'll always be a hefty percentage of what you will do as a business owner.

Much like your business plan, your marketing plan should be a simple, one-page outline of what your goals are and how you plan to achieve them. Keep in mind that it's not written in stone; it's a guide to get you under way and to keep you on track. You can make changes and adjustments at any time down the road.

Get out some paper and a pen and get ready to create your plan. The first thing I want you to do is review this chapter's list of marketing methods. On your sheet of paper, list the ones that seem appealing to you, that you'd be excited about trying. List as many as you'd like.

Next, you'll have to do some research. For each method you selected, get some specific costs. Call your local papers, talk with a representative from a mailing list company, get quotes for printing business cards—whatever you need to do to determine a price range for this method. Then calculate how many paying clients you'll need to cover the cost of that marketing effort. Also, how much time will it take for you to implement this method? Finally, on a scale of 1 through 10—with 10 being great excitement—rate each method depending on how interested you are in trying it. This is important, because even though a certain method may be more time consuming or costly, if you believe in your heart that it's the way you want to go, that's where you'll work the hardest.

I strongly support going with your gut.

Now go through your list and choose your top three methods based on budget, time, and interest. These will be the ones you include in the first round of your marketing efforts.

How will you know if you're marketing effectively? Bringing in more money than you're spending is the first criteria. Also, look back at the income you hoped to make per year. Break that number down into monthly amounts and see if you are on target. Once you're about six months into a particular marketing strategy, take the time to evaluate its effectiveness.

Advertising and marketing are both constants in this industry. There'll never be a time when you're not doing one or the other if you're interested in keeping your business alive. It can be challenging, expensive, even downright exhausting to keep the pipeline full with potential clients. Still, the longer you are out there sharing your talents, enthusiasm, and energy for what it is you love to do, the more the word spreads and the business shows up.

Sample Marketing Plan and Evaluation

On the following pages, there are examples of sample plans and how you might fill out your Marketing Plan Worksheet and Marketing Evaluation Tool.

Marketing Plan Worksheet

What are your goals?

I am committed to organizing _____ (#) hours per week.

I will do this by _____ (date).

I am committed to creating _____ (#) paid speaking engagements each month, by _____ (date).

How do you plan to get there?

I am excited about the opportunity to market in the following ways (list your top three):

Method 1: _____

Target clients: _____

Estimated cost in dollars: _____

Estimated cost in time: _____

Action items: _____

_____

_____

Method 2: _____

Target clients: _____

Estimated cost in dollars: _____

Estimated cost in time: _____

Action items: _____

_____

_____

Method 3: _____

Target clients: _____

Estimated cost in dollars: _____

Estimated cost in time: _____

Action items: _____

_____

_____

Visit www.BalanceAndBeyond.com for downloadable version.

Marketing Plan Worksheet

What are your goals?

I am committed to organizing _____*20*_____ (#) hours per week.

I will do this by _*Dec. 15, 2011*_ (date).

I am committed to creating _*3*_ (#) paid speaking engagements each month, by

*Oct. 31, 2011* (date).

How do you plan to get there?

I am excited about the opportunity to market in the following ways (list your top three):

Method 1: _*Advertise in local resource directory.*_

Target clients: _*Local homeowners, stay-at-home moms.*_

Estimated cost in dollars: _*$1,800/year.*_

Estimated cost in time: _*4–6 hours.*_

Action items: _*Design ad – Get pricing and compare – Get samples of several resource directories – Ask about their circulation, locations, etc. – Call other advertisers in the directory and ask their feedback on responses they've had.*_

Method 2: _____

Target clients: _____

Estimated cost in dollars: _____

Estimated cost in time: _____

Action items: _____

_____

_____

Method 3: _____

Target clients: _____

Estimated cost in dollars: _____

Estimated cost in time: _____

Action items: _____

_____

_____

Marketing Evaluation Tool

Method used: _____

Actual cost in dollars: _____

Actual cost in time: _____

Number of clients secured because of this method: _____

Number of speaking gigs obtained: _____

Other opportunities that came from this effort: _____

_____

Do I consider this method to be effective?   ☐ Yes   ☐ No

Explain:

_____

_____

_____

_____

_____

What would I do differently next time?

_____

_____

_____

_____

_____

Visit www.BalanceAndBeyond.com for downloadable version.

Marketing Evaluation Tool

Method used: _Advertising in local resource directory._

Actual cost in dollars: _$2,150 (needed assistance designing ad)._

Actual cost in time: _About 4–6 hours._

Number of clients secured because of this method: _12 calls in the first 3 months, and 2 clients signed on._

Number of speaking gigs obtained: _4 people booked me for upcoming speaking gigs._

Other opportunities that came from this effort: _One corporate customer called; we're talking about a lunch-and-learn session in the fall._

Do I consider this method to be effective?   ☑ Yes   ☐ No

Explain:

The two clients who signed on each took a package of hours and paid for the cost of the advertising and then some. With all the other activity so far, this is paying off big time!

What would I do differently next time?

I would run the ad just slightly larger; it seemed to be lost on the page next to the other ads.

Colleagues' Corner

Ruthann Betz-Essinger, owner, Just Organized, LLC

First hurdle: "Fear of failure." Having an MBA and a strong marketing background was a benefit and a curse at the same time for Ruthann. Pressure to succeed was at times crippling. She knew not only from experience, but also from teaching it to her students, that "most businesses fail. I don't want to be another statistic. I even pretended not to be in business for a while because I was so afraid of saying I was in business if it was not going to make it. Once I stopped pretending to not be in business and just got on with doing it, it was pretty easy."

Marketing successes: "I go to a business networking group called BNI (Business Networking International). Not only have I gotten referrals, I've learned how to get up and talk short and sweet about my business. You get about thirty seconds to tell what it is you do, and you learn pretty quick how to get to the point. I have also met other entrepreneurs at the weekly meetings; in fact, an IT guy was the one who suggested I create packets of time to sell to my clients instead of an hourly rate. Great resources and support from others in business for themselves."

Level of satisfaction: Ruthann proudly proclaims, "I still love my job as much today as I did when I started back in 1999. I'm as happy as a clam!"

07 Products

TV has done a lot to introduce professional organizing to the general public. However, the way in which our field is represented is a bit misleading. Makeover shows run thirty to sixty minutes and wrap up an entire roomful of organizing from start to finish in that time. We know this is not possible in the real world, but your clients, who may be fans of these shows, will often be astounded when you tell them it could take ten to fifteen hours to finish each room. Unlike real life, reality TV shows have editors who can boil down sixty or seventy hours of work into a thirty-minute episode!

Shopping for the products alone can take several days to get right. Most clients are anxious to see all those beautiful bins, baskets, containers, and furniture in place and working smoothly. Explaining that product purchasing is one of the last things on the to-do list can be a challenge. You, too, might get inspired and want to start buying bins and baskets. Restrain yourself! I have learned from experience that end results always look very different from my initial vision for the space. Remember that you first have to ascertain what your clients need—not what they *want*. In addition, it's only going through all their excess stuff that will enable you to design the perfect system for them. So don't be afraid to take your time before heading out to buy organizing products.

I always recommend setting up temporary storage using whatever boxes and bins clients have around the house to see if a particular organizing system will work properly before purchasing the final products. I like to let clients work in their temporary system for several days or even weeks to see if it's right, and to make any needed adjustments. Only then do I start thinking about purchases. I take some photographs of the areas we are working on, and off I go to do some "shopping" in search of the perfect product. On my next visit with the client, I review the options I have found; together we decide on the one we think will work the best.

This chapter will cover the many aspects of this product search, including pricing items, buying them, and getting them to your clients.

Good Things Come to Those Who Wait

I once had a client who was chomping at the bit to purchase a particular videotape holder. I asked her to please wait. Well, she became very upset. She really wanted this piece, she was convinced it was going to work for her, and it was currently on sale. I stood firm.

Several weeks later, when this client and I started organizing her videos, we ended up housing all of them in the basement in an industrial-type file unit. Why? She had more than 400 videos, and that was after her elimination process! There were family videos, kids' videos (she had five children), and so on, and so on. Clearly she couldn't store them all in her small living room.

This solution fixed all kinds of issues. Every Friday night became video night, when the kids all went to the basement and chose three videos to keep in their room for the week. They stopped making duplicate and triplicate purchases because they now knew where the videos were, too. Best of all, clutter was eliminated throughout the house.

By the way, the container that my client had wanted so badly held only 175 videos. It wouldn't have been much of a bargain!

Finding Products

An organizer looking through a good product catalog is like a kid in a candy store. Whenever my husband catches me looking through a catalog, I just tell him, "It's research!" I use that same excuse as I roam through the aisles at stores such as Bed Bath & Beyond, Target, and one of my favorites, the Container Store. These are wonderful places to wander through to keep your mind filled with the latest and greatest in storage and organizing. Keeping aware of both new and old items is important when you're working with your clients. They are counting on you to find the perfect solution to their organizing dilemmas; the more knowledge of products you have, the better.

Here are some product-buying tips to get you started:

- Try to find products at three price points: low, medium, and high.
- Of course, you want the best quality you can find for the price as well.
- Find out how returns are handled.
- Will there be any shipping and handling fees?
- How long will it take to obtain the product?
- Be sure to think about your clients' decorating style as well.

The Internet

Shopping online for products is the ultimate convenience. You just type a description of what you're looking for into a search or shopping engine, and within seconds you've got many (often too many!) options to choose from. If you're not sure what exactly you're looking for, search more general terms and a multitude of storage solutions are presented for you. For instance, if I search for "garage storage," my results include everything from bike racks to floor coverings to tool storage. It can provide you with many ideas for a particular project.

The advantages of online shopping are myriad. Your search is simplified; you can print out information on specific products to show your clients; products are delivered right to your door, or your clients'; and in most cases no sales taxes are charged. On the downside, you cannot check the products' quality, returns are sometimes complicated, and there are often hefty shipping and handling charges. Shopping on the Internet gets easier the more you do it, because you become familiar with online stores that carry quality products and have customer-friendly return policies.

Catalogs

Like the Internet, catalogs provide a multitude of solutions. The search isn't nearly as easy as on the web, of course, although you can review items in detail in the comfort of your home—or bring the catalog with you to your clients' home. On the other hand, you often have to look through many catalogs before finding the item you want; returns can be cumbersome; and taxes, as well as shipping and handling charges, can be high.

Once you start catalog shopping, you end up receiving so many in the mail that keeping them organized is a challenge. At one time I had a hanging file cabinet to hold my favorites—more than a hundred of them! Unfortunately, this wasn't a good system; when working with a client I would grab several catalogs, sometimes ten or fifteen at a time, and when I got home it seemed too tedious to file each one back away. I ended up simply storing my favorites in a large basket that I would occasionally go through, weeding out older versions. Internet shopping has generally replaced catalog shopping for me these days; I keep only a few special catalogs around.

Stores

You can also shop the old-fashioned way, in stores. Just as when you shop catalogs, of course, it's easy to get distracted with other interesting products while in search of a particular item. This is great in terms of research and knowing where to find these items for future projects—but it does cut into your time for the project at hand. It's nice to be able to touch the product to check its quality and sturdiness. There are no delivery charges (unless you can't fit it in your car), and because you're able to check out the quality, shape, and size of the product so thoroughly, there's typically less chance you'll need to return it. On the flip side, it takes a lot of time to visit different stores in search of the perfect product.

I make an effort to examine products and test them out as best I can while I'm in the store. As we all know, they don't make things like they used to. If I'm going to recommend products to my clients, I want to feel confident about the quality. So

---

Recommended Resources

Some of my favorite product sites:

- The Container Store (www.containerstore.com)

- Stacks and Stacks (www.stacksandstacks.com)

- Solutions (www.solutions.com)

- Organized A to Z (www.organizedatoz.com)

See appendix C for an entire listing of great sites.

opening and closing doors, lifting tops, and turning things over—or under—are all helpful ways to determine how well a product will withstand everyday use.

Evaluating Products

Like many consumers, I love gadgets. But there are good gadgets and bad gadgets. So many organizing products claim to simplify, organize, and systematize our stuff that clients often think they've only to purchase one to miraculously clear out their clutter. In fact, these gadgets most often are the *cause* of their clutter. For instance, battery organizers allow clients to snap the batteries into place by size. They're neat little doohickeys, but unfortunately most clients just don't have time to take batteries out of their original containers and place them neatly in this tray. Even if they do, they probably have more C batteries than the gadget holds, which leaves all those extra C batteries floating around the closet or drawer for clients to wonder, *Is this a good battery or not? Why is it not in my gadget?* But there is an easier, more efficient way of storing batteries: a square container labeled batteries that allows the client to store many different types of batteries, in various amounts, all together.

Your client is paying you the big bucks to identify products that are helpful and useful, not gadgets that will end up being more trouble than they're worth. My theory, repeated often through this book, is the simpler, the better. If it has a lid, get rid of it; if it has a door, pull it off. Less is more in most cases.

If I think a product might be useful to my clients, I typically buy it for myself and try it out for a while. I ask myself: *Is it truly easy to work with? Does it make sense? Do I use it?* The best part of this is that you can put some great products to use in your own home, all in the name of research! Speak with your accountant, too, because some or all of these may be tax-deductible expenses.

As an organizer you should be able to identify the pros and cons of particular products quickly. Suggesting a product to clients that ends up not working well, or is of poor quality, reflects badly on you. There have been many products that I thought for sure would work out great...and they were disasters! That's why it's good to know the pros and cons before recommending anything. Try it out, or have a friend or family member do so.

How do you go about evaluating products? What makes a product good, bad, or otherwise? There are several questions you should consider:

- It is easy to use?
- Will it hold up to repeated use?
- Does it do what it says it can do?
- Are there too many parts?
- Does it take too many steps to use it?
- Is it a good design, or does it make the job more cumbersome?

I once tried out a three-shelf toy storage unit; it also has angled bins that can be pulled out for use. What I found was that the bins are too small to store any one category of toy, they're awkward and cumbersome to pull out, and labels just don't seem to stick to them. Ultimately toys simply get thrown into whatever bin is available. The bins then get overfull and impossible to put away, so they're left on the floor. These are the kinds of product issues you want to know about *before* recommending anything.

Door Prize

I was working in the rooms of two young children. They each had a closet with 3-foot-wide doors that opened outward. These were little kids—four and seven years old—and they had a terrible time maneuvering the big doors whenever they had to pull something out or put something away. I suggested removing the doors altogether. The mother at first thought I had lost my mind, but after I talked with both her and the kids about it, we decided to try it out for a week. We removed the doors, which we stored in the basement. We organized the children's clothes, creating lower bars that they could reach and spots for all their important kid things.

When I made my next visit, the mother reported that it had worked like a charm. The younger one had even started to dress herself more often, because Mom could set out on the lower bar outfits for her daughter to choose from. To this day, more than four years later, the doors remain in the basement. The closets have been "prettied up" so they look great, and the children are much better about picking up their stuff. My client also mentioned that it's a topic for discussion at many a coffee klatch: "That crazy organizer who told me to take the closet doors off!" She reports that everyone laughs—and then she tells them how well it's working out. Soon enough, more closet doors are coming off!

Function Versus Form

I believe that the most important criterion in evaluating a product is: *Does it do what clients need it to do?* Nevertheless, the product should be appealing and stylish as well. Of course, certain products that won't be seen, such as kitchen cabinet pullouts or drawer organizers for the office, aren't as big a deal as baskets or bins for the living room or decorative containers for the office or bedroom and such.

When it comes to style, take your cue from clients. Browsing through catalogs might help you learn what style most appeals to them and find products they like. When organizing a closet, for example, you can buy matching hangers in plastic, wood, and metal; there are even different colors of wood to choose from. Talk with your clients and choose the style that most appeals to them. These are the finishing touches that clients will be excited about.

Before calling you, your clients have likely searched through catalogs and purchased many different products. They will be frustrated at having already spent time and money in a failed attempt to get themselves organized. So they're counting on you to work some magic—finding the right product to do the right job at the right price and with style.

Getting Products to Your Client

There are many ways to get products to your clients, and no right or wrong ways to do it. Let's look at some of your options.

Shopping *with* the Client

I recommend that you start your shopping at "home" first—the clients' home, that is. Look around for whatever baskets and bins they previously purchased in attempts to get organized; chances are you'll end up with a multitude of options. I've talked about the importance of setting up temporary organizing systems prior to making purchases. Using items that clients already have in their homes saves them time and money—and you already know that the products appeal to them aesthetically, given that they're the ones who bought 'em in the first place!

If you shop on the Internet or in catalogs, introduce your clients to some of your favorite hot spots. If you end up purchasing a product, clients can use their own credit card and have it shipped right to their door. (Make sure you review the return policies with clients before making the purchase.) Clients have the benefit of you being right there helping them make good choices. By thinking out loud as you

A Few of My Favorite Things

IKEA's file cabinets

I like the "Effectiv" grouping. The drawers extend out fully; they hold up under repeated use and can tolerate a good amount of weight. **www.ikea.com**

Ultimate Document Desktop Organizer

A great way to store many frequently used lists or documents, keeping them at your fingertips and organized. **www.ultoffice.com**

Cubi Triple Decker Desk Organizer

The drawers pull completely out for ease of use; it can be labeled on the front of the drawers, and it's stylish. Great desktop piece. **www.levenger.com**

The Portable File Cart

Need quick access to files and form isn't critical? These file carts (z-line Alero mobile 2 tier file cart, black) are awesome. Priced right, they make using your files easy and convenient. You can roll them up to any work area and get started. **www.staples.com**

Panef, white silicone

Use it on all surfaces to lubricant instantly eliminate rubbing, squeaking, and sticking. My clients think I've worked magic! This product is VERY hard to find. Visit my website to purchase directly from me.

Plastic drawer boxes, varying sizes

These are essential to creating a finished look in a drawer with undergarments, socks, T-shirts, etc. They are inexpensive but create a polished finish to any organizing job. **www.stacksandstacks.com**

Three-bin laundry

I like the ones that are sorter permanently attached to the frame, not hooked on, because they are easiest to use. It's an inexpensive product, and clients will wonder how they did without it. **www.stacksandstacks.com**

evaluate the product, you're giving folks a lesson in the fine art of evaluation! This is also a good opportunity to double-check the measurements you've taken to make sure the product will fit the space.

I have offered to meet clients at a particular store to search for particular items. We've sometimes spent our entire session time at a store, or we have made purchases and then gone back to the house to put the items into use. I find that clients like to shop with me, because they are getting an education as to where to find the best products, and they get to see into the mind of an organizer when it comes to evaluation.

Shopping *for* the Client

If I'm not sure what a client might need, or if I don't have particular products in mind, I may do some investigative work between visits. I search on the Internet, in catalogs, and in stores. If a good-looking product is on the Internet or in a catalog, I will typically show it to clients, either via e-mail or at our next visit; they can make the decision to purchase or not. If the product is available for me to pick up and bring to the client and I am reasonably sure it will suit their needs, I do so and have it ready for our next visit.

There are two ways to charge clients for a product search: by the hour or through markups on products that you bring to them. If my searches are specific to one client and one particular item, I will charge the client for my time. However, if the search is really an educational experience for me and has introduced me to new locations and options for future work, I do not charge my client for this time. Rather, I charge them the cost of the product, with a markup. Most clients are so happy that I've brought them a great product to try out, they're willing to pay the higher price.

I once worked on a kitchen with a client who was in a hurry to get the job done: She was eight months' pregnant. Taking a chance, I purchased many kitchen cabinet organizer items, most of which I had used before on other kitchens, but several that were new and unfamiliar to me. At my next visit we tested them out, putting some into place and deciding to return others to the store. She was thrilled and didn't hesitate to pay my 40 percent markup after I explained that it took care of any credit card charges, my time, and my travel costs. I took a risk in this case, but I recommend you discuss your intentions with clients beforehand. If they aren't comfortable paying a markup on a product that they can go out and buy themselves, save yourself the time.

Determining markup on items is variable. It depends on the price of the item and what you feel comfortable charging. Typically, I mark up products that cost less than $150 at 30 to 40 percent. I consider higher-priced items individually, taking into account my time, travel, any shipping fees, and any other expenses I might encounter.

If you will be reselling any items to a client—file folders, drawer organizers, kitchen cabinet pullouts—with a markup, you will need to obtain a resale certificate. Search the web for "resale certificate" and your particular state, then complete a simple form and submit it (see chapter 3). This puts the state on alert that you will be collecting sales tax for products you're selling. You must then file a quarterly report letting the state know how much you have collected and that you will be sending the money in. States handle this tax very differently, and the rules change so rapidly that it's hard to discuss them here with accuracy. The fastest way to find the right forms is to search the Net under your state name and "tax forms," then look for the business section.

Clients Shopping on Their Own

You can also have your clients purchase products themselves. The good part about this method is clients feel involved in the process, and they can find products that meet their aesthetic needs. The downside: Some clients struggle with the task. No matter how much information you give them regarding the size, shape, and features of the products they need, they just don't have as much experience as you

---

Shopping Tips

Whether you are shopping with clients or for clients—or even sending them out on their own—here are some basic tips:

- Keep the shopping specific to your project's particular needs.
- Bring with you a detailed list of what you're looking for, what you are going to store in it, and any style likes and dislikes.
- Also bring the measurements of the space you're working with. A small drawing or photograph of the space is very helpful.
- Carry with you a tape measure, pen, pad of paper, and digital camera.
- Make sure your vehicle is large enough to carry home the product, and emptied of other items.
- Evaluate products for quality, ease of use, and style.

at evaluating products. They usually end up with something that almost works, or almost fits, which could leave the system you designed in shambles. Asking clients to shop works best if you give them very specific parameters—size, function, drawers, no drawers—or better yet, product numbers, along with the locations where they can find what they need.

Each client's expectations will be different. Some want nothing to do with purchasing products and are willing to pay if you do the shopping; others want to go out and shop on their own. There is no right or wrong here; whatever you and the client work out is fine. But do keep in mind the end goal, which is a space that functions smoothly and looks fantastic.

Product Design and Development

Besides guiding your clients toward purchases, you can also provide products you've made yourself. You can create booklets, e-books, workbooks, audiotapes, videotapes, CDs, DVDs, viral videos, newsletters, and starter kits all related to organizing. When you're just starting out, this may be a challenge, but as your business grows and you find yourself repeating similar information to client after client, you may find it valuable to simply record this information for everyone.

Think about topics like these:

- How to Organize Your Kitchen
- Creating an Awesome File System
- Garage Cleanup and Clean-Out
- Getting Your Teen Ready for College
- Hassle-Free Holidays

Whenever you speak somewhere, record your performance on video and audio if possible. If you can only audio-record it, it's still worth doing. These tapes can be sold if they are packaged properly, and also used to create booklets and e-books. Videos are a bit more of a challenge. You want the quality to be professional, and the cost of hiring a crew may be more than you can afford right now. Once you've perfected a workshop or presentation that you believe there is a market for, however, get it taped and ready to sell. The average cost of taping a two- to five-hour presentation is around $1,200. To have this turned into a sellable product—one that's professionally edited and produced—ranges from $200 to $800 or more. That's a hefty investment, but if it provides you with a marketable product, it can begin earning you money right away. Anytime you speak, offer it for sale in the back of the room. Also, clients who aren't ready to hire you for one-on-one organizing work may opt to purchase your tapes to get started.

When it comes to designing new products for market, there's opportunity all around. As you get to know the market, you may find ways to improve upon existing products. Over the years organizers have designed and developed many products, then collaborated with manufacturing companies to get them out to the general public. If you come up with a great idea, go for it! (See "Product Design and Sales" in chapter 8 for more.)

Product Sales and the Internet

Selling products through your website is a good way to earn additional revenue. Setting up affiliate programs with sites offering organizing products will allow clients to purchase the items through your website, with you getting credit for the sales. Learn about affiliate programs by going to the site you hope to create a relationship with. Typically you'll find an affiliate button on the bottom of their page. Read through the company's agreements. Once you set up these relationships, you can begin placing pictures of particular items directly on your site, or you can simply include a link to the affiliated site. Anytime a client clicks through from your site to theirs, it's recorded, and you get credit for any purchases made.

● ● ●

As you can see, there are many options for selling, designing, and profiting from organizing products. Clients are eager to get started buying a variety of products, and it will be up to you to steer them in the right direction. The products will be there long after your work is done, so make sure each one represents you well in quality, function, and form.

08 Ready, Set, Grow!

Now that you own your own (thriving!) business, what do you want to do with it? This chapter will identify many of the issues you'll face when deciding whether or not to grow your business.

Starting with a very basic one: Why grow your business? What *is* growth, anyway—gathering more clients? Hiring other organizers? Public speaking? Bigger web presence? Taking products you've designed to the market? And how will you know when it's the right time to grow? Not only do I want to help you figure out your motivation for growing the business, I want to give you a realistic idea of what kind of commitment you will be making if you decide to take this exciting step.

Why Grow the Business?

Before I begin to share with you the hows of growing your business, I want to encourage you to think about the whys. There are many ways in which you can expand, and it's important to know exactly what you're getting into if you decide this is the next step for you.

Are you looking for greater income? Recognition in the industry? New and exciting adventures? What makes you think you need to grow your business? Do you have so many clients you're turning new requests down? Are you so out of balance everywhere in your life that if you took on any new clients, it would just break the proverbial camel's back? Are you tired of the mental drain and physicality of the job—sorting, cleaning, climbing, bending—and ready for a change? Maybe you want to expand your business because you think that's the natural next step. Isn't that what businesses do, get bigger? What if you're enjoying your business just the way it is? Do you really *need* to grow the business? Sit down, ask yourself these questions—and be as honest as you can with your replies.

Reasons to Grow

- **Greater income:** Well, who wouldn't want to increase their income? But don't forget that along with more money typically comes more work and more expenses. I suggest that you don't expand your business solely for a bigger paycheck. Once you're knee deep in new responsibilities and challenges, you'll want more reward than just a few dollars.
- **Greater challenge/new adventure:** Perhaps you are interested in a new adventure. You started this business awhile ago and it's been moving along splendidly, with an increasing flow of clients. You feel confident in the work you do—and now the entrepreneurial spirit in you wants more. More of the same, more of something new to keep you interested and excited about your business in general. This is great! And if this is you, hold that thought and we'll get to the new adventures in a bit.
- **Recognition in the industry:** You've been organizing and enjoying yourself, and now the thought of getting involved with the real movers and shakers of the industry appeals to you. If you're ready for the limelight, then by all means follow your heart and get ready to shine.
- **Lifestyle change:** You love the bins and baskets and files and piles, but now your home life has changed, and you need to make adjustments to your work life. Great: As a home-based business owner, you're perfectly poised to take advantage of the flexibility and control you already have.

The Ideas File

Now would be a good time to create an Ideas File if you don't already have one. If you're anything like me, you'll find yourself coming up with ideas or thoughts about new growth or revenue opportunities for your business—at any time night or day! It's good to have a file or notebook handy to capture these ideas. When you sit down to brainstorm possible growth avenues, you can pull out this file and evaluate some of your ideas.

What Direction Do you Take?

Once you're clear that you do want to grow, and why, the next question is: How? There are many ways to expand that will fulfill your ambitions, but it's important that you know the pros and cons of each and the impact they will have on your income, lifestyle, workload, and more. Lucky for you, I've tried just about all of them.

Workshops and Seminars

Early on in my career, I thought about hosting workshops and seminars for the general public. With so many disorganized people out there, I figured, I was sure to fill a room with paying attendees. So I found a venue, determined the price I would charge, created a list of dates and topics, and went to work on my computer creating flyers, sign-up forms, mailers, you name it. I purchased a mailing list of 5,000 names in my local area to send my workshop schedule to. I sent out about 600 mailers, posted flyers at local coffeehouses and supermarkets, and sent information to my clients.

After all that effort I got three paying attendees and held only one workshop. It was a hefty investment of my time and money with very little return. In fact, I actually lost money when you take into account the fees for the room, mailing list, and postage as well as the hours I spent designing flyers and doing other promotion work.

Workshops and seminars are certainly a great way to get your name out there and grow the business. Unless you have an unlimited budget to market and fill a room, however, you'll need help. I suggest you partner with a local business to create a win–win situation. For example, I have recently partnered with local assisted-living facilities to use their conference space for workshops. They want individuals to come to their facilities as a way of introducing the general public to all they have to offer; I need a site for workshops. We each do our own marketing, flyers, mailings, and local postings, and we've been successful at filling the room. In the middle of my workshop, I leave about fifteen minutes for the manager to come in and talk about the facility. It works out great for everyone: The facility gets the message out, I have a space to make my presentations, and I can charge the attendees less for the conference because the facility is not charging me a fee to use the room. So when considering workshops, look for a reliable partner who will benefit from your success as much as you will.

Speaking—Corporate Gigs

After my first unsuccessful attempt to grow, I realized that if I could increase my speaking engagement fees, it would bring in extra money—and more than likely provide me with private clients as well. I first thought about my network: Who could I ask about speaking at their company? I called previous clients who worked at appropriate companies and let them know I was now doing "lunch-and-learns," a term I heard from a friend. (The company hires you to come in and speak for about an hour as their employees eat lunch.) I knew I could do this since I had been speaking in front of groups large and small for the past year. I put together some topics and continued spreading the word. I got a call from a local company that had heard about me through a friend and wanted to see what topics I could speak on. She loved the list I sent her:

- Clutter to Clarity
- Eliminating Procrastination
- Paperwork Power
- Time to Spare
- 4 Steps to Organizing Anything

She then asked the more interesting question: "What do you charge for a one-hour lunch-and-learn?" It was my first time doing this, so I didn't have a set rate schedule. I blurted out a number and held my breath.

"Well," she said, "that's a little more than our budget allows, but let me check with my boss and see what she says." I thought for sure I'd blown it and was very upset about not having been prepared. I got off the phone and immediately called a colleague—she's in a different industry but also does lunch-and-learns—and picked her brain. I determined that my rate had actually been right on target.

The next day, since I hadn't heard back from the company, I called and said to my contact, "I am very interested in doing business with you and your firm, and I don't want price to keep us from working together. If you need me to make an adjustment to meet your budget, please let me know." She appreciated my call and was happy to hear that I was flexible.

The next day she called me back: They'd decided to hire me for three topics, and at the rate I'd originally quoted! I was thrilled to have broken into the world of corporate speaking. I found out several months later that I'd gotten the job because my contact was impressed that I had been so honest about being new to the corporate speaking world and was willing to work with them on fees. I have continued to do work with this firm over the past five years, and have also gotten other speaking engagements thanks to their referrals.

People love to hear organizers talk about their work. There's something about the topic of organizing, time management, and paperwork management that captures their attention. If public speaking is something you love to do, this could be a very profitable way to go about growing your business. Prepare your topics, create a fee schedule, and begin making inroads.

My "A" List

I am often asked about organizers "in my area" if I am speaking in an area I don't practice. I have compiled a list of Professional Organizers whom I recommend. I have entered into a verbal referral agreement with these organizers, and get a 10 percent commission on any business my "A" list organizers get within a year of being contacted by someone specifically mentioning my name, my company's name, or one of my presentations.

Referral Arrangements

As time went on and I continued to book more speaking engagements, a funny thing happened. I started getting more clients! The more I spoke, the more people were inspired to hire organizers and get organized. I was thrilled that I was having such an impact on my audiences. Only problem was, I didn't seem to have the time to fit them into my schedule. What was I to do? I began reaching out to other organizers and offering to give their names to prospective clients.

Well, you could imagine what their response was. "Sure, send them on over!" I eventually created a formal referral agreement so that I could receive a commission for referrals. Bingo, another revenue stream for my business.

And yet, I *still* had more clients than I could reasonably fit into my schedule. They say necessity is the mother of invention. Well, I needed to find more organizers, and if I couldn't find them, maybe I could create them.

Training and Apprenticing New Organizers

I started training organizers several years ago. I was motivated for two reasons: I had too many clients to handle on my own or to refer to others, and (even more important) I found out I was pregnant! I realized that it wouldn't be long before climbing, bending, squatting, and stretching were going to get a lot more difficult. One night before going to bed, I sat quietly with my thoughts. *How can I stay at home with my new baby, still help my clients, and make money at the same time?*

What happened the next morning was nothing short of astounding. I woke up, got myself a cup of coffee, and went to check my e-mail. There it was, a message from a young woman who had seen an article about me several months prior. She had been thinking about becoming a professional organizer and wanted to know if I was interested in hiring an apprentice. I looked around the room as if there were a hidden camera somewhere. Could this possibly be the answer to my question? Three weeks later I was sitting in a room with six women, training them in the art of professional organizing.

I was sure my ship had come in. I sent organizers out to work with clients while I sat back, put my feet up, and raked in all the cash. Well, the warning should be, don't sit back too far or your chair will flip over! The next paragraph is one I wish I'd read back then.

First and foremost, remember your business plan. Since my guess is that you're reading this book to get your business started, your business plan currently captures your start-up ideas; you've left the growth ideas for when you're ready. Well, when and if you do decide it's time to grow the business, don't forget to revisit your business plan. You can still use the same questions and simple format, but know that everything gets more complicated once you take on employees. Doing the office work, marketing, payroll monitoring, legal minutiae, and more quickly becomes a blur when you're busy training new employees. I found this out the hard way. Because I was so busy managing and training my new organizers, the pipeline for new business went dry in a hurry. Suddenly I couldn't provide the new organizers with enough work. They became discouraged, and some began looking for clients on their own.

This is where that business plan starts to come in handy! You will have the greatest chance of success if you think about growth ahead of time. How fast you'll grow, how many organizers you'll want, how many client hours you'll work, how much money you'll need for the increased marketing, how many speaking engagements you'll want to book...think through all of this and more.

Let me tell you more about what you'll need to be prepared for. The legal and accounting issues expand exponentially when you begin to work with employees or independent contractors.

Hiring Checklist

- Have the employee complete a W-4 form.
- Obtain his or her Social Security number.
- Conduct a background check.
- Set up payroll with your accountant or through your accounting software.
- Determine a formal method of reporting hours worked.

Employees

Employees are people on your payroll and for whom you withhold taxes; you also control where, when, and how they do their jobs. Apprentices and people that you mentor are considered employees in the eyes of the IRS, so I'll refer to them that way. Taking on employees doesn't mean that your business structure has to change— even if you are a sole proprietor. I do recommend, however, that you contact your insurance agent and make any necessary adjustments in your coverage.

Agencies such as OSHA, Workers' Compensation, and the Labor Board all have requirements you must meet with regard to safety in the workplace, discrimination, wages, and more. All are critical. Your local office supply store is a great resource for computer software that includes all state and federal policies and forms; you might also check out Socrates (www.socrates.com) and FindLaw (www.findlaw.com). I recommend you do some research in this area, check out your particular state's policies, and then consult with an attorney. Penalties and fines could be levied against you as the employer if you do not adhere to these requirements.

Again, if this is the direction you'll be taking your company, there is much to be said for consulting with experts. Even if you have been maintaining your own financial information, you will want to consult with an accountant just to set up everything properly so that you can maintain it throughout the year.

You're also going to have to train your new employees, which takes time and energy. And what's to keep folks from coming to you for this training and information—then striking out on their own? After all, with books like this one, can't anyone start their own organizing business? Yes, and this is why I strongly recommend you establish a noncompete agreement with any new organizers who come on board. A noncompete will prohibit new hires from working for any of your current clients and marketing their services to any contacts they made through working with you, at least for a period of time.

There are two kinds of employees: those who just want to work for you, and those who want to eventually go into business for themselves. First let's talk about new organizers who have no interest in starting their own business. These are great employees to have. They work what's called a per diem schedule: Much as in an on-call arrangement, you call them in when you need them. You might ask them to help you with a specific client for a brief period, even only for a day or so. Organizers like these are typically interested in part-time work that will fit in with their current lifestyle or family needs.

Then there are those new organizers who are entrepreneurs at heart. They're looking for some apprenticeship and mentoring, but they'll be starting their own businesses as soon as they get their sea legs. I would much rather know this up front so I can offer a win–win situation. A win–win goes something like this: I train them in the art of professional organizing, and they commit to working for me for a specific period of time at a specific rate. For instance, I had several new organizers who were interested in working with me to get more experience in the organizing industry. I required that they pay for the training and work a minimum of twelve hours per week for six months. Of course, the hours were flexible, but the idea was to get them to commit to a time frame. This allowed me to go out and get business, knowing I had the staff to fill the need.

It's a delicate balance. I recently spoke to someone who is doing this very successfully. She did, however, tell me that she has one person taking care of the financial and legal part of the business, and another dealing with marketing; she focuses solely on mentoring and training. All this support keeps the business running smoothly and the clients coming in. She also realized that it was the mentoring she enjoyed the most. I like to train, but find the mentoring in the field to be too time consuming and not much fun. We're discussing how to create a win–win situation together.

Independent Contractors

Independent contractors are different from employees. They are individuals or business entities that are not employed by you, so *they* determine the wheres, whens, and hows of their jobs. They invoice you for the work completed and are responsible for dealing with their own taxes. You might use an independent contractor when you don't want to hand over a client as a referral, but you still need an experienced organizer to pinch-hit for you. Maybe it's an area of organizing you're not fond of or qualified to provide; maybe you need time away from the business for personal reasons.

If you send out employees or independent organizers, you can expect to receive anywhere from 50 to 70 percent of the fees. For instance, if the rate you charge the client is $65, it would be reasonable to pay your independent contractor or employee anywhere from $20 to $30 per hour. Your percentage covers the advertising and other business expenses that you incur in the procurement of the client.

There are many advantages to working with independent contractors. You would still maintain the client in your book of business for any future projects. In addition, you can send contractors to work immediately with clients; there is much less management of the actual organizing work, if any; and if you are comfortable with your contractors' philosophy and methodology, it could be a match made in heaven.

The downside? Independent contractors typically cost more per hour due to their experience; also, you run the risk of losing business, just as if you were training a new employee. If you are introducing professional organizers to clients and contacts, what's to keep them from "stealing" business? To avoid this, have a frank conversation and set up a win–win situation—maybe an increased hourly rate for them, or a percentage for any hours the clients book beyond the original hours. It's also a good idea to put your agreement in writing. This agreement should include a noncompete clause that prevents your contractors from working with anyone who has been a client of yours, at least for a period of time.

I learned about the importance of getting agreements in writing the hard way. I had someone working for me who, during her visits with a client, spoke with the client's husband and was eventually hired to work with his company. While it wasn't

Support Groups

Getting support from other organizers or entrepreneurial support programs as you grow your business can be invaluable. Claire O'Connor from Enchanted Home says, "I would not be where I am today without my various teams over the years. Check out Barbara Sher's writing on the topic at www.shersuccessteams.com or www.enchantedhome.net." You can request Claire's booklet *Dream Team: How to Create Structured Support for Getting What You Want* to help you set up your own support team.

technically the client she solicited work from, it made me reluctant to use her with any future clients.

Even though the possibility exists of losing business to an independent contractor or an employee, I think the benefits outweigh the risks. You have a greater potential to serve more clients, which in turn will generate more business. You must ensure that any independent contractor who's out there representing you and your company is capable and qualified to do the job. Your integrity and credibility are on the line.

A Word About Integrity

I believe integrity is the backbone of any successful business. Lose it, and it will come back to bite you. If something you're doing doesn't feel on the up-and-up, it probably isn't, and you should reconsider your actions. If it's something you've already done, then clean it up however you can and move on. Do you owe someone a referral fee? Have you blatantly used information that was someone else's and not given credit? Acting without integrity is one sure way to slow the growth of your business and to lose credibility in the profession.

Growing your business with employees and other organizers can be lucrative and rewarding. However, it will certainly increase your workload and your need for supportive services. If you are up for this challenge, remember to get out your business plan and detail how you will handle the growth. Set it all down on paper before you begin, and you'll save yourself heartaches and headaches along the way.

I realized, after many experiments, that not only did I have no desire to manage employees or contractors, but the timing was all wrong for my family and myself. I needed to find yet another way to continue making money doing something I loved, but with limited increase in workload.

Ways to Increase Your Income
Increasing Your Rate

Working with other organizers may be the most challenging way to grow your business. Now let's talk about one of the easiest: increasing your hourly rate. You've been in the business for some time now and your skills have increased, so why not your fees?

Increasing your rate just $10 per hour, based on 20 hours per week with clients, will net you $800 more per month. Not too shabby! Your hourly rate could also be boosted if you begin contracting with more corporate clients. Traditionally, corporate clients pay higher rates; bringing on even one or two will boost your income significantly.

Raising your rates can be done gradually over time, or you can just make the adjustment immediately for any new clients who come on board.

Increasing Your Hours

Perhaps you've been working only eight to twelve hours a week and have been reluctant to schedule more. Maybe now is the time to step it up. It does increase your workload, and may cramp your lifestyle a bit, but it will certainly increase your income.

Is there room in your schedule to see more clients? Can you see them in the evening or on weekends? Can you handle two clients a day? Trying this growth strategy requires deciding what you are willing to sacrifice in exchange for seeing more clients. Maybe if you had help in other areas, such as bookkeeping, marketing, or making client calls, you would free up more time to work with clients. Hiring an assistant for office work and handling other business details may be all you need to make this profit-boosting option work for you.

Writing for Profit

Are you a good writer? Then you may have opportunities to grow your business using your talent writing newsletters, booklets, training manuals, magazine and newspaper articles, maybe a magazine or newspaper column of your own—even a book. If this thought gets your juices flowing, then break out your laptop and head to the local coffee shop. Your income, should you follow this option, will depend on the type of writing you do and the contracts you sign or how you go about selling what you wrote (I'll talk about that in the next section). The lifestyle or workload impact from this option can be as varied as the income.

When I was approached to write this book, I was thrilled, knowing that it was a wonderful opportunity to grow my business. I also believed that it would allow me to spend more time at home with my girls, which it did. As far as my two girls go,

I certainly was able to spend more time with them at home, being very creative to schedule work time between diapers, sleepless nights, and my husband's full-time job. It's been a rewarding experience, but not nearly as simple as I had first thought. Now that they're "big girls" (all of 5 and 6 years old and in school), it allows me to again sit and look at my business and see what new direction I'd like to take now, if any.

Make sure to sell anything you write on your own website, and begin setting up those strategic alliances I talked about earlier to start generating more visitors. Also, the many different sites that carry organizing products may be willing to list your booklets, e-zines, and more for visitors to purchase.

Product Design and Sales

Increasing product sales is another way to increase your profits. List products for sale on your own website. You'll also want to create affiliate programs with sites that have good merchandise; any purchases made through your website will give you credit for the sales. This can be fairly lucrative. If other organizers are working for you and doing the same thing, your profits will continue to climb.

Don't forget creating products yourself as a growth avenue. Writing is one such product, of course; e-books, booklets, and books can be sold to the general public to help them get organized. Other products you can create: videos, DVDs, CDs, and even computer videos if you are technically savvy. These products can be sold at all of your speaking engagements, at trade shows, on your website, and through other sites or selling services such as Amazon.

The Organized Organizer

As mentioned earlier in this book, the original organizer bag I found was perfect for all the supplies I needed on client visits. Knowing how difficult it was to find the "perfect" bag, I saw a need and jumped in. I used my bag as a jumping off point and made all the little changes I new would make that bag better. And viola, my very first organizing product, The Organizer's Work Bag, is now available. Check out my website to order yours!

Product development and sales can be a way to supplement your income or even become your primary income generator. Some professional organizers have been in the trenches for a long time and find themselves ready for a change of pace—and eager to share the knowledge they've gained over the years. Informational products are great value-adds for clients, profit earners, and marketing tools all in one. Having a specialty can be especially helpful here. For instance, if you enjoy helping people move from their homes or offices, you can put together a moving guide and advertise in a catalog that sells boxes and moving supplies. There are also many opportunities to write about yourself and get noticed in magazines, newspapers, and newsletters. (See chapter 6 for all the details.)

You know all those gadgets and gizmos out there that make organizing so much fun? Well, where do you think they come from? Someone must have had the idea, along with the initiative and drive to bring it to market. If you have the idea and the know-how, you can design, develop, and deliver to market your very own organizing gadget. Of course, this option does come with a hefty price tag. Quite a bit of groundwork needs to be done—you'll need to research similar products, find a good patent attorney, look for a company that will assist in putting a prototype together, test the product in the market, and more. There are services out there, though, that can help with the entire process. For starters, check out the U.S. Patent and Trademark Office (www.uspto.gov) and Invention Home (www.inventionhome.com).

Phone Organizing

Can you organize over the phone? I was skeptical at first, but once I tried it I was hooked. I was approached by Dorot University—a "university without walls"—to conduct teleconference classes, mostly for the elderly and disabled. I set up a filing course that was one hour long, once a week, for four weeks. It was a great experiment in whether organizing can be taught over the phone, and as things turn out, it can! I realized there could be a market for this. I came up with a simple one-hour, four-week plan to reach clients who couldn't afford my on-site hourly rate or who were located somewhere other than my working area.

It worked great. I'd make an initial assessment by looking at photographs or videos of the client's space. Then we would set up a time to talk, after which they'd get off the phone and get to work. We scheduled hourly check-ins so I could keep tabs on their progress. At the end of the session, I assigned them homework to do before our next visit. The clients who had the technology sent me e-mail photos of their progress, and that was our starting point for our next call. This system was a great way to make money when I needed to be home with my growing family.

> **Recommended Resource**
>
> Two great resources for group teleconferences are www.freeconference.com and www.freeconferencecall.com. The companies help you set up the conference, and all you pay is the cost of the call.

Is It the Right Time?

By now you know why you want to grow, and you've decided how you want to grow. Next question: Is this the right time to grow? This is a very personal question to answer. Timing is everything, they say, and when it comes to growing your business, it couldn't be more true. I have shared with you bits and pieces of my growing pains. Without a guide, I basically made things up as I went along and was never fully aware of what I was getting into until I was already in the middle of it. Hopefully the information in this chapter has inspired your entrepreneurial spirit—but also encouraged you to plan ahead before taking any action.

Take it from me: Before making any decisions about growing your business, sit down and reevaluate your business plan. Then take this business plan and line it up next to your life plan. Do you have a life plan? Most of us don't. A life plan identifies important accomplishments, achievements, and characteristics of the life you'd love. I find that the bigger my personal life gets, the more I have to be very specific as to what it is I truly want for myself, my girls, my marriage, my family, my spiritual life, my career, and so on. All of these will be affected when you choose to start or grow your business.

Early in this book we talked about the costs of doing business, and I mentioned five of them: physical, mental, emotional, spiritual, and financial. Well, I'd like you to create goals or intentions for six months, one year, three years, and five years in each of these areas. This process will help you gain some perspective on where your work fits into the overall picture. I was a nurse for many years, and I never once heard a dying patient say, "I wish I'd made more money," or "I know I could have done more speaking gigs." Not once.

I sometimes get caught up in the excitement of starting something new and may even launch a project before sitting down to ask myself, *Is this something I really want to do?* It's been a hard lesson to learn, but since the birth of my two daughters, I'm realizing that I don't have to do everything that comes my way, or that I am capable of doing. Starting something that is not suited to your home or family life can have devastating effects on everyone. It puts tension on marriages, it leaves children wondering where Mom or Dad is, it leaves you burning the candle at both ends just to get things done. Timing is critical for the success of your business, so make sure you talk with everyone who will be affected by your choices before jumping in. You'll be glad you did.

Things to think about: What does your financial picture look like? Can you afford to make changes that may cost you money up front? How stable is your home life? If your heart and mind are preoccupied with the failing health of a parent, or the trouble you're having with your teenager, or the fact that you just moved to a new neighborhood, how do you expect to have the energy and focus you will need to make changes in your work life? Be honest with yourself now, or be stuck in reality later. There is always time to grow. It may be now; it may be six months from now; it may be a year. Do yourself a favor: Whenever the idea of growing your business strikes, take a deep breath, reread this chapter, and begin to craft a plan. I know you'll do great.

Conclusion

I'd like to personally congratulate you for your commitment to starting your own business. It's not easy, but it definitely is rewarding. I have enjoyed every step of the process, and each day I find exciting new reasons for being in business for myself. I have never been bored, and I can grow or slow my business exactly as I wish to work it around my lifestyle. I have enjoyed meeting other business owners along the way and suspect you will, too, as your business grows. Remember, this business is yours, and you get to design it as you see fit.

One of the greatest advantages of a home-based business is that you are the decision maker. You are the one who decides where the business is going, how fast, under what conditions, and in what direction. All entrepreneurs—all successful entrepreneurs—thrive on the excitement inherent in the new and unknown. They are quick thinkers and problem solvers. With the information you've read about starting, running, and growing your own professional organizing business, you're well on your way.

Appendix A:
Websites and Resources

For Organizing

- National Association of Professional Organizers (NAPO): www.napo.net
- Professional Organizers in Canada (POC): www.organizersincanada.com
- Professional Organizers Web Ring (POWR): www.organizerswebring.com
- The David Allen Company: www.davidco.com
- Home Made Simple: www.homemadesimple.com
- Fly Lady: www.flylady.com
- Saving Dinner: www.savingdinner.com
- Time to Organize: www.Time2Organize.net

For Small Business

- Business Owner's Toolkit: www.toolkit.cch.com
- Business registrations: www.irs.gov/businesses/small
- Chamber of Commerce: www.uschamber.com
- Legal advice: www.nolo.com; www.business.gov
- National Association for the Self-Employed: www.nase.org
- National Association of Home Based Businesses: www.usahomebusiness.com
- Small Business Administration: www.sba.gov
- Tax forms: www.irs.ustreas.gov
- Toast Masters: www.toastmasters.org
- Wellness Possibilities: www.wellnesspossibilities.com
- Working Solo, Inc.: www.workingsolo.com

Women Owned

- Powerful You: www.powerfulyou.com
- Cashman Consulting: www.cashmanconsultingllc.com
- Savor the Success: www.savorthesuccess.com
- National Association of Women Business Owners: www.nawbo.com
- Conscious business: www.kathysmylymiller.com

Important IRS Forms (Available at www.irs.ustreas.gov)

- Form 1040, Individual Income Tax Return
- Form 1040-ES, Estimated Tax for Individuals
- Form 4562, Depreciation and Amortization
- Form 8829, Expenses for Business Use of Your Home
- Schedule A, Itemized Deductions
- Schedule C, Profit and Loss from Business
- Schedule D, Capital Gains and Losses
- Schedule SE, Self-Employment Tax

Appendix B: Recommended Reading

For Organizing

ADD Friendly Ways to Organize Your Life, Judith Kolber and Kathleen Nadeau

One Thing at a Time, Cindy Glovinsky

Mom, Inc., Neale S. Godfrey

Repacking Your Bags, Richard J. Leider and David A. Shapiro

Clear Your Clutter with Feng Shui, Karen Kingston

Confessions of an Organized Homemaker, Deniece Schofield

Feng Shui: Harmony by Design, Nancy Santo Pietro

Getting Organized, Stephanie Winston

Organize Yourself!, Ronni Eisenberg

Organize Your Office!, Ronni Eisenberg

Organizing for the Creative Person, Dorothy Lehmkuhl and
   Dolores Cotter Lamping

Lose 200 Lbs. This Weekend: It's Time to Declutter Your Life, Don Aslett

Clutter Be Gone!, Don Aslett

Clutter's Last Stand, Don Aslett

Taming the Paper Tiger at Home, Barbara Hemphill

Taming the Paper Tiger at Work, Barbara Hemphill

File...Don't Pile, Pat Dorff

For Time Management

How to Have a 48-Hour Day, Don Aslett

The Personal Efficiency Program, Kerry Gleeson

Time Management, Marshall Cook

Prioritize, Organize: The Art of Getting It Done, Jonathan Clark and Susan Clark

The Seven Habits of Highly Effective People, Steven Covey

For Small Business

The E Myth, The E Myth Revisited, Michael E. Gerber

The Big Leap, Gay Hendricks

The Toilet Paper Entrepreneur, Mike Michalowicz

Mastering the Rockefeller Habits, Verne Harnish

The One Page Business Plan for the Creative Entrepreneur, Jim Horan

Your Limited Liability Company: An Operating Manual, Anthony Mancuso

Everything I Needed to Know About Business I Learned in the Barnyard, Don Aslett

The Magic of Thinking Big, David J. Schwartz

Big Things Happen When You Do the Little Things Right, Don Gabor

For Surviving in the World of Owning Your Own Business

All in the Name of Love, Barbara Smyly and Glenn Smyly

You Can Heal Your Life, Louise Hay

Your Money or Your Life, Joe Dominguez and Vicki Robin

Do What You Love, the Money Will Follow, Marsha Sinetar

Taming Your Gremlin: A Surprisingly Simple Method for Getting Out of Your Own Way, Rick Carson

Refuse to Choose, Barbara Sher

The Power Is Within You, Louise Hay

Live the Life You Love, Barbara Sher

The Best Year of Your Life, Debbie Ford

Self-Employed Tax Solutions, June Walker

For Public Speaking Help

What's Your Story, Craig Wortman

Speak Up, Don Aslett

Speak from the Heart, Steve Adubato

Talking the Winner's Way, Leil Lowndes

Appendix C:
Product Catalogs and Websites

My websites: www.BalanceAndBeyond.com
                    www.WellnessPossibilities.com

A Good Steward: (908) 647-1856; www.agoodsteward.net

Ballard Designs: (800) 367-2775; www.ballarddesigns.com

California Closets: (888) 336-9709; www.calclosets.com

Container Store: (800) 733-3532; www.containerstore.com

Crate & Barrel: (800) 323-5461; www.crateandbarrel.com

Day Runner: (800) 232-9786; www.dayrunner.com

Day Timer: (800) 225-5005; www.daytimer.com

Exposures (photos): (800) 572-5750; www.exposuresonline.com

Franklin-Covey: (800) 842-2439; www.franklincovey.com

Get Organized: (800) 803-9400; www.shopgetorganized.com

Hold Everything: (800) 421-2264; www.holdeverything.com

Ikea: (800) 434-4532; www.ikea.com

Levenger: (800) 544-0880; www.levenger.com

Lillian Vernon: (800) 545-5426; www.lillianvernon.com

Lizell: (800) 718-8808; www.lizell.com

Martha Stewart Living: www.marthastewart.com

Mead/At-a-Glance: (800) 323-0500; www.ataglance.com

Mobile Office Outfitter: (800) 426-3453; www.mobilegear.com

Office Depot: (800) 685-8800; www.officedepot.com

Photo storage ideas: www.photostodvd.com; www.vialta.com

Planner Pads: (402) 592-0676; www.plannerpads.com

Pottery Barn: (800) 922-5507; www.potterybarn.com

Reliable Home Office: (800) 869-6000; www.reliable.com

Rubbermaid: www.rubbermaid.com

Sky Mall: (800) SKY-MALL; www.skymall.com

Smead: (651) 437-4111; www.smead.com

Space Saver: (800) 849-7210; www.spacesaver.com

Stacks and Stacks: (877) 278-2257; www.stacksandstacks.com

Staples: (800) 333-3330; www.staples.com

Storage Store: (800) 600-9817; www.thestoragestore.com

Storage Works: (403) 990-0839; www.storageworks.com

Taylor Gifts: (800) 829-1133; www.taylorgifts.com

Ultimate Office: (800) 631-2233; www.ultoffice.com

Q: How much should I charge?

A: By far this is the most frequently asked question. You should consider four factors when pricing yourself: level of experience, type of service being provided, area of the country, and confidence level. You're new, so your experience is about what you're bringing to the profession, your background, your passion, your ability to give the clients what they're looking for, etc. You have to measure the value of this for yourself. The type of service includes in-home hourly, in-office hourly, and corporate presentation. All command a different fee structure. The national average for in-home hourly is $55 to $85 per hour, which leads into the next factor: the area of the country. Do some research to determine the current average in your area. And then there's the last, but most influential, factor: confidence. If you find your area supports a rate of $65, are you going $20 under or over that? Where are you on the continuum of this? Keep in mind it's hard to raise rates too quickly, so whatever you start at you'll have to work up slowly. If it's too low to support your financial needs, keep this in mind. Use the formula in the book to help get those answers. Then use these parameters to finalize.

Q: What type of training is required to become a professional organizer?

A: There are no required programs or formal training to become a professional organizer at this time. There are, however, training programs offered by the professional associations as well as seasoned organizers. Anyone with the passion and skills to assist others in creating more organization and systems in their lives can become a professional organizer.

Q: Where can I get experience working with clients?

A: Many organizers have worked with family and friends to gain experience—in fact, this is how some have discovered that they have a knack for this kind of work. You can work with more experienced organizers as an apprentice, assistant, or subcontractor to gain valuable client experience as well. There are also ways to volunteer, donate, or discount your rates in order to gain experience. Yet another method may be to exchange services with someone, such as a web designer.

Q: How much money did you need to start your business?

A: The average start-up costs range from $ 4,000 to $15,000, which includes a computer, website design, and more. While there are items that are critical to have in the beginning, others can be purchased as you go along. Establishing yourself as a business is relatively inexpensive. Business cards and a phone line are usually the first items on the list. Marketing and advertising would be the first real major investment, along with any training or coaching in organizing skills or business management. Speaking with many organizers, I found that most had no budget in mind when they started; they used the extra cash they had on hand and a credit card or two, growing the business as their income grew.

Q: What's the best way to get started?

A: The best way to get started is to first determine what your goals are. Are you looking for extra cash doing something you love? Are you looking to start and grow your own business? Do you need to support a family with this income? Are you looking to work full-time or part-time? Are you prepared to be an entrepreneur? Your answers will help you decide whether you want to start a business or perhaps seek out other organizers and offer your skills and talents to them. If you're unsure, maybe you want to start working with another organizer first and revisit these questions after a period of time. Once you have a strong commitment to a plan, then it's time to do some research. Books like this one are your first step if it's a business you plan to start and grow yourself.

Q: What types of forms do you need to get started?

A: My paperwork philosophy is: Keep it simple, very simple. Most individuals are coming to you because they are overwhelmed with stuff, and that includes paper.

I have two operating forms when it comes to my residential clients. The first is a one-page assessment of what I believe it will take to get their space in order, along with the cost and some tips to get started. This form also lists pertinent information including my phone number, a plan of attack, and my working agreement (cancellation policy, payment requirements, and the like)—all short and sweet. The second is a work record. This records the dates, times, and content of our work sessions. I keep this record in the client folder that I maintain and review with clients at each visit.

Q: Do you bring the supplies to the client or do they buy them?
A: Both. When I'm working with clients, I prefer to set up temporary storage to see if certain systems will work. Once we're satisfied with these solutions, I help clients identify the permanent products they need. Some clients feel comfortable searching and purchasing products on their own; others want the organizer to do it for them.

Q: How much money can I make at this? Can I make a living doing this?
A: Income varies dramatically. The number of hours you plan to work, your hourly rates, and the ways in which you grow your business all have an impact on your bottom line. Are you going to be working with corporate clients or residential? The hourly rates are different. Are you going to be networking to find clients or running splashy ads? The costs, again, vary widely. Will you be hiring subcontractors to do the work for you and have several of them out there? Will you be working part-time hours when your children are in school? All will factor into your income potential. Based on the average hourly rate for organizing services of $55 to $150, grab a calculator and play around with the numbers; you'll get a feel for what your potential is. Some organizers have ventured into to the professional speaking world and increased their earning potential dramatically.

Q: Should I be prepared to take credit cards?
A: This is something that you can add as you go along. The ability to take credit cards makes it easier for clients to pay for larger hourly packages, if that is something you offer. Still, I accepted only checks or cash for my first four years in business and it was never an issue, even with the larger package rates. I now accept credit card payments through my website as well.

Q: What do you do when clients cancel an appointment?

A: During my first visit with a client, I review the plan of how we will work together, including my cancellation policy. Most clients understand that when they cancel and I cannot schedule another client, my income is affected. When you're working week by week, billing the client as you go, charging for missed or canceled appointments is difficult. Sending someone an invoice for hours you weren't there may create resentment. If they've paid you up front for hours, however, reducing their balance of hours is easier. I reduce their hours by 50 percent of the scheduled appointment time. For instance, if we had an appointment on the books for four hours, and they canceled that day or the evening before, I charge them for two hours. This is also only after giving them one grace cancellation and reviewing the cancellation policy with them. I have charged only a handful of clients for this, and even then only once per client—they catch on quick.

Q: Are there training classes available?

A: There are many seasoned organizers in the industry who have valuable experience to share. This information can save you time, money, and energy. Attending a training workshop can provide valuable lessons from the field, along with specific time-saving tips, techniques, and tools for setting up your business and working with clients. You gain comfort and confidence by seeing what others do and realizing how much you can in fact bring to the table for your clients. Attending a training workshop also allows you to answer the question, "How did you learn how to do this?" when a potential clients asks.

Choosing the right training experience for you is important. Do you want to attend a two- or three-day workshop that includes hands-on organizing training? Do you want to attend a tele-class, listening in and working with printed materials? Do you feel the need to work one-on-one with a coach or consultant in the field? Does this trainer offer apprenticeship programs? Might you be hired as a subcontractor after the training? There are many opportunities for you to gain valuable training because there are many seasoned organizers out there. Seek out the training that suits you best. Interview trainers and find out their philosophy, their style of organizing, their success in the business, and how they operate.

Q: **Should I join a professional association—and if so, which one?**

A: Joining a professional association is helpful in a variety of ways. If it's one for professional organizers, such as NAPO or POWR, you gain valuable information about the industry and instantly have colleagues to share experiences with and gain knowledge from. If the association is focused on marketing—say, a chamber of commerce or networking group—you'll hopefully gain clients, but you may also find other entrepreneurs, usually in your local area, with whom you can share and get support from.

There are many associations and groups out there. My suggestion is to visit their meetings and ask questions. Get a feel for the energy and think about whether it's a group you would be excited to be a part of, and a positive force in your business. Most have yearly or monthly dues, so be sure you'll receive value for your time and money commitment.

Q: **What type of business entity should I set up?**

A: The majority of professional organizers run their businesses as sole proprietorships or LLCs. Each type of business entity has advantages and disadvantages, as well as certain requirements on a state and federal level. You'll want to evaluate these requirements and determine your best course of action with the help of an accountant or attorney, especially if you have other tax or legal concerns.

Q: **What type of marketing or advertising seems to bring in the most clients?**

A: There are a variety of ways to gain exposure and obtain clients—so many, in fact, that you will want to focus your marketing efforts in an area that suits your personality and your business. I happen to love making presentations in front of groups. Speaking at local women's clubs has actually given me almost 95 percent of my client base, including corporate clients. Maybe you enjoy writing? Articles in local papers or submissions to newsletters would be a great opportunity. Do you love to network? Then business groups or associations may be the route for you. Advertisements are another option. Find a periodical that targets your market and create or have created an ad that is clear, concise, and to the point. When it comes to marketing and advertising, the "spend big, get big results" theory doesn't always work. Stay within your budget with something that suits your personality and interests; then track your outcomes and find out what works for you.

Q: Do I need a web page?

A: Yes and no. It all depends on the plan for your business and what your goals are. If you're interested in working for another organizer as a subcontractor and aren't looking to drum up your own clients, then a website probably isn't a necessity. If you are starting business on your own and plan to grow your client base and possibly sell products or offer workshops, however, then you will absolutely need a place to lay out this information for prospective clients. The web is a great place to share your rates, what types of work you do, and maybe some before-and-after photos—in most cases for less money than a brochure or any printed material would cost, and in a format that can be changed whenever you like. A website isn't something you need to get started in the business, but it certainly helps give you a more professional appearance.

Q: Where do you find organizing products for your clients?

A: Everywhere! Of course I have some favorite spots, such as Stacks and Stacks, the Container Store, and others. Catalogs and the Internet are invaluable, too. Still, I believe good products are those that exactly fit your clients' needs. You don't have to use products conventionally, either, as long as they work.

As an organizer you are always looking at systems and ways to improve them. I find that I evaluate gadgets and gizmos almost instinctively as I walk through stores or browse through catalogs. Essentially, products are all around. Staying open to new and ingenious ways to use items is part of the expertise our clients pay us for, and for most of us it's fun, too!

Appendix E:
Useful Forms

With everything else on your plate to get your business started, there's no reason to reinvent the wheel when it comes to the forms you'll need when working with clients. The forms I have created are simple, easy to use, and all inclusive for your start up needs.

You can use the following forms as a guide in creating your own, or you can go to my website and download them for free as PDF's or as Microsoft Word documents. Use the forms as is and then, as time goes by, modify them to fit your style and specialty of organizing.

[Your Logo Here]

ASSESSMENT VISIT/WORKING AGREEMENT

Name: _____

Date: _____

Address: _____

Phone: _____

Estimate of work schedule: _____

_____   _____

_____   _____

_____   _____

_____   Totals: _____

Hourly and package rates:

Tips to get started: _____

_____   _____

_____   _____

_____   _____

Plan of action: _____

Working agreement:

Phone call confirmation: Unless otherwise stated, I will not call to confirm appointments. If you need to change or reschedule your appointment time, it is your responsibility to contact the office and do so.

Cancellation policy: Cancellation of a scheduled appointment with less than 48 hours' notice will be billed at 50 percent of the agreed-upon rate or time scheduled.

Travel rates: Travel greater than 45 minutes in either direction will be billed at 50 percent of the agreed-upon rate.

Business Name   **Phone**   **Website**

Visit www.BalanceAndBeyond.com for downloadable version.

[Your Logo Here]

CLIENT INTAKE FORM

Name: _____

Date: _____

Address: _____

Phone: _____

How did they hear about us: _____

General phone intake: *Here is where you write down parts of your initial conversation with clients. Do they have children? Do they work or are they stay-at-home parents? What's the reason for their call? What's their primary area of interest? Any information that allows you to get to know the client would be captured here.*

You can also jot down what you've discussed: rates, packages, time frames, and so forth. You will review this with them at your assessment visit.

If you schedule an assessment visit at this point, write it down here and in your calendar.

Directions: _____

_____

_____

General client/family description: *This is where you write down your impressions after your assessment visit. When they call back to schedule future appointments, you'll want to recall any conversations you had at your assessment.*

_____

_____

_____

Plan: *Record your initial plan for the clients. At this point you will have left an assessment form with them, but you need to recall what you wrote down. You can also record their available days and times here.*

_____

_____

_____

Visit www.BalanceAndBeyond.com for downloadable version.

[Your Logo Here]
WORK RECORD

Client name: _____

Address: _____

Phone number: _____

Payment record:

Rates quoted to client:

Package hours: _____

Date: _____ Time: _____ Project: _____ # Hrs. Wrkd: _____ # Hrs. Left: _____

Date: _____ Time: _____ Project: _____ # Hrs. Wrkd: _____ # Hrs. Left: _____

Date: _____ Time: _____ Project: _____ # Hrs. Wrkd: _____ # Hrs. Left: _____

Date: _____ Time: _____ Project: _____ # Hrs. Wrkd: _____ # Hrs. Left: _____

Date: _____ Time: _____ Project: _____ # Hrs. Wrkd: _____ # Hrs. Left: _____

Date: _____ Time: _____ Project: _____ # Hrs. Wrkd: _____ # Hrs. Left: _____

Date: _____ Time: _____ Project: _____ # Hrs. Wrkd: _____ # Hrs. Left: _____

Date: _____ Time: _____ Project: _____ # Hrs. Wrkd: _____ # Hrs. Left: _____

Date: _____ Time: _____ Project: _____ # Hrs. Wrkd: _____ # Hrs. Left: _____

Date: _____ Time: _____ Project: _____ # Hrs. Wrkd: _____ # Hrs. Left: _____

Date: _____ Time: _____ Project: _____ # Hrs. Wrkd: _____ # Hrs. Left: _____

Visit www.BalanceAndBeyond.com for downloadable version.

[Your Logo Here]

INVOICE

Date: _____

Client: _____

Address: _____

Invoice #: _____

Description of services: _____

_____

_____

Fee: _____

Total: $ _____

Payment terms: *Payment is due first day of service (larger packages may be split up into two payments, if you'd like).*

Congratulations on your commitment to getting organized. We're happy to be assisting you along your journey!

Thank you,

Your name
Business name
Business address
Phone number

Visit www.BalanceAndBeyond.com for downloadable version.

Marketing Evaluation Tool

Method used: _____

Actual cost in dollars: _____

Actual cost in time: _____

Number of clients secured because of this method: _____

Number of speaking gigs obtained: _____

Other opportunities that came from this effort: _____

_____

Do I consider this method to be effective?   ☐ Yes   ☐ No

Explain:

_____

_____

_____

_____

_____

What would I do differently next time?

_____

_____

_____

_____

_____

Visit www.BalanceAndBeyond.com for downloadable version.

Marketing Plan Worksheet

What are your goals?

I am committed to organizing _____ (#) hours per week.

I will do this by _____ (date).

I am committed to creating _____ (#) paid speaking engagements each month, by

_____ (date).

How do you plan to get there?

I am excited about the opportunity to market in the following ways (list your top three):

Method 1: _____

Target clients: _____

Estimated cost in dollars: _____

Estimated cost in time: _____

Action items: _____

_____

_____

Method 2: _____

Target clients: _____

Estimated cost in dollars: _____

Estimated cost in time: _____

Action items: _____

_____

_____

Method 3: _____

Target clients: _____

Estimated cost in dollars: _____

Estimated cost in time: _____

Action items: _____

_____

_____

Visit www.BalanceAndBeyond.com for downloadable version.

Mileage Record

Date	Destination	Starting Mileage	Ending Mileage	Total Miles

[Your Logo Here]

Photo Consent

Date: _____

We are very proud of the organizing work we have done with you and would like to include it as a part of our work history. There is no identification, reference to locations, or any information of a personal nature included when photos are used.

I (We), _____, do hereby consent to give [Company Name Here] the right to use my photographs for reproduction purposes in the promotion of their organizing services. These purposes include, but are not limited to, teaching booklets, slides, overheads, posters, presentations, and Web site. It is also my understanding that following the initial use of such photographs, I may instruct [Company Name Here] to discontinue their use at any time in the future. I have read this release and fully understand its content.

Name: _____

Signature: _____

Address: _____

_____

Guardian: _____
(if under 18)

Referral Record Log

Client name: _____   Client name: _____

Referred by: _____   Referred by: _____

Referral gift: _____   Referral gift: _____

Date sent: _____   Date sent: _____

Project description: _____   Project description: _____

Client name: _____   Client name: _____

Referred by: _____   Referred by: _____

Referral gift: _____   Referral gift: _____

Date sent: _____   Date sent: _____

Project description: _____   Project description: _____

Client name: _____   Client name: _____

Referred by: _____   Referred by: _____

Referral gift: _____   Referral gift: _____

Date sent: _____   Date sent: _____

Project description: _____   Project description: _____

Client name: _____   Client name: _____

Referred by: _____   Referred by: _____

Referral gift: _____   Referral gift: _____

Date sent: _____   Date sent: _____

Project description: _____   Project description: _____

Client name: _____   Client name: _____

Referred by: _____   Referred by: _____

Referral gift: _____   Referral gift: _____

Date sent: _____   Date sent: _____

Project description: _____   Project description: _____

Appendix F:
More Creative Ideas

Need some inspiration? Take a look at some solutions that have worked for my clients.

Before

After

Before

After

Before

After

Before

After

Before

After

Index

confidentiality, 112
Contact Plus Professional, 34
Container Store, 166, 207
corporate clients, 35, 190
corporation, 46
costs, 12
coupon packs, 146
creating balance, 31
creative ideas, 218
credit cards, 121, 204

D
debit cards, 51
deductions, 56
diner place mat ads, 133
direct-mail letters, 146
dish stackers, 173
donation sites, 75
door prize, 170
drawer boxes, 172
dressing for work, 88
DVDs, 177, 191

E
e-books, 177, 191
education, 61
800 phone numbers, 26
EIN (Employer Identification Number, 53, 54
Eliminate (in L.E.A.S.E.), 73
e-mail contacts, 36
emotional costs, 15
emotional problems (in M.E.S.S.), 69
emotions of clients, 126
employees, 185
employee tax, 55
Employer Identification Number, 53
Ennis, Debbie, 31, 138
entrepreneurial traits, 4
Equalize (in L.E.A.S.E.), 76
equipment, office, 21
essential items, 68
estimating the job, 118
evaluating (organizing step), 76
experience, xii, 61
e-zines, 148

F
family meetings, 122
fax lines, 27

Faye, Ellen, 115
file folders, 22, 80
filing cabinets, 78
filing system, 31
filing tips, 33, 81
financial records, 50
first visit back with a client, 125
flyers, 147
forms, 208
4 Steps to Organizing Anything, 63
4 Steps to Organizing Anything, assessing, 65
4 Steps to Organizing Anything, evaluating, 76
4 Steps to Organizing Anything, implementing, 72
4 Steps to Organizing Anything, planning, 71
freebies, 148
free work, 5
frequently asked questions, 108, 202
friends-and-family rate, 96

G
gift certificates, 17, 131
goals, 193
graphic artist, hiring, 140
growing your business, 179
growing your business, timing of, 193
guarantees, 123

H
handouts, 148
health insurance, 49
hiring checklist, 185
home office deduction, 56
home office space, 23
homework, 101
hourly rate, 94, 189, 204

I
Ideas File, 180
IKEA file cabinets, 172
implementing (organizing step), 72
income potential, 16
income tax, 54
increasing your hours, 190
increasing your rate, 189
independent contractors, 187
insurance, 47
integrity, 189
Internet, 153

About the Author

Dawn Noble, president and founder of Balance & Beyond, is a registered nurse and professional organizer. Dawn established Balance & Beyond to assist individuals in learning the basics of de-cluttering, organizing, and time management, helping them create more satisfying, healthier lives. She has coached many individuals and small-business owners to create more efficient, more productive envi-  ronments. She has trained and educated individuals in the art of professional organizing and coaches new entrepreneurs in the art of establishing and growing their small businesses.

Dawn has spoken publicly to hundreds of local groups and clubs, as well as to many corporate clients. Dawn has been quoted and written about in *Parenting* magazine, *Family Circle* magazine, and a variety of popular newspapers and magazines. Dawn currently lives in Butler, New Jersey, with her two girls and husband.